W9-BRM-281

# Holidays
# Family Nights Tool Chest

## Creating Lasting Impressions for the Next Generation

# Jim Weidmann and Ron Wilson
## with Kurt Bruner

Cook Communications

Heritage Builders

This book is dedicated to Cheryl, my wife and best friend; to my kids, Breanna, Nathan, and Lauren, who have brought me such great joy; and to my God, who makes life one great family night.

—*R.W.*

Cook Communications Ministries, Colorado Springs, Colorado 80918
Cook Communications, Paris, Ontario
Kingsway Communcations, Eastbourne, England

HERITAGE BUILDERS/FAMILY NIGHTS TOOL CHEST—HOLIDAYS
© 1998 by Jim Weidmann, Ron Wilson, and Kurt Bruner

First edition 1998

Edited by Steve Parolini
Design by Bill Gray
Cover and Interior Illustrations by Guy Wolek

ISBN 1-56476-737-X

Printed and bound in the United States of America
04 03 02 01 00   5 4 3 2

*Heritage Builders/Family Nights Tool Chest—Holidays* is a Heritage Builders book. To learn more about Heritage Builders log on to our website at: www.heritagebuilders.com

# Contents

*The Heritage Builders Series*

Designed to motivate and assist families as they become intentional about the heritage passing process, this series draws upon the collective wisdom of parents, grandparents, church leaders, and family life experts, in an effort to provide balanced, biblical parenting advice along with effective, practical tools for family living.

Kurt Bruner, M.A.
Executive Editor
Heritage Builders Series

# ☙ Introduction

There is toothpaste all over the plastic-covered table. Four young kids are having the time of their lives squeezing the paste out of the tube—trying to expunge every drop like Dad told them to. "Okay," says Dad, slapping a twenty-dollar bill onto the table. "The first person to get the toothpaste back into their tube gets this money!" Little hands begin working to shove the peppermint pile back into rolled-up tubes—with very limited success.

Jim is in the midst of a weekly routine in the Weidmann home when he and his wife spend time creating "impression points" with the kids. "We can't do it, Dad!" protests the youngest child.

"The Bible tells us that's just like your tongue. Once the words come out, it's impossible to get them back in. You need to be careful what you say because you may wish you could take it back." An unforgettable impression is made.

Impression points occur every day of our lives. Intentionally or not, we impress upon our children our values, preferences, beliefs, quirks, and concerns. It happens both through our talk and through our walk. When we do it right, we can turn them on to the things we believe. But when we do it wrong, we can turn them off to the values we most hope they will embrace. The goal is to find ways of making this reality work for us, rather than against us. How? By creating and capturing opportunities to impress upon the next generation our values and beliefs. In other words, through what we've labeled impression points.

The kids are all standing at the foot of the stairs. Jim is at the top of that same staircase. They wait eagerly for Dad's instructions.

"I'll take you to Baskin Robbins for ice cream if you can figure how to get up here." He has the attention of all four kids. "But there are a few rules. First, you can't touch the stairs. Second, you can't touch the railing. Now, begin!"

After several contemplative moments, the youngest speaks up. "That's impossible, Dad! How can we get to where you are without

touching the stairs or the railing?"

After some disgruntled agreement from two of the other children, Jacob gets an idea. "Hey, Dad. Come down here." Jim walks down the stairs. "Now bend over while I get on your back. Okay, climb the stairs."

Bingo! Jim proceeds to parallel this simple game with how it is impossible to get to God on our own. But when we trust Christ's completed work on our behalf, we can get to heaven. A lasting impression is made. After a trip up the stairs on Dad's back, the whole gang piles into the minivan for a double scoop of mint-chip.

Six years ago, Jim and his wife Janet began setting aside time to intentionally impress upon the kids their values and beliefs through a weekly ritual called "family night." They play games, talk, study, and do the things which reinforce the importance of family and faith. It is during these times that they intentionally create these impression points with their kids. The impact? The kids are having fun and a heritage is being passed.

# ❧ intentional or "oops"?

Sometimes, we accidentally impress the wrong things on our kids rather than intentionally impressing the right things. But there is an effective, easy way to change that. Routine family nights are a powerful tool for creating intentional impression points with our children.

The concept behind family nights is rooted in a biblical mandate summarized in Deuteronomy 6:5-9.

> *"Love the LORD your God with all your heart and with all your soul and with all your strength. These commandments that I give you today are to be upon your hearts. Impress them on your children."*
> *How?*
> *"Talk about them when you sit at home and when you walk along the road, when you lie down and when you get up. Tie them as symbols on your hands and bind them on your foreheads. Write them on the doorframes of your houses and on your gates."*

In other words, we need to take advantage of every opportunity to impress our beliefs and values in the lives of our children. A growing network of parents are discovering family nights to be a highly effective, user-friendly approach to doing just that. As one father put it, "This has changed our entire family life." And another dad, "Our investment of time and energy into family nights has more eternal value than we may ever know." Why? Because they are intentionally teaching their children at the wisdom level, the level at which the children understand and can apply eternal truths.

# ☙ truth is a treasure

Two boys are running all over the house, carefully following the complex and challenging instructions spelled out on the "truth treasure map" they received moments ago. An earlier map contained a few rather simple instructions that were much easier to follow. But the "false treasure box" it lead to left something to be desired. It was empty. Boo Dad! They hope for a better result with map number two.

**STEP ONE:**

Walk sixteen paces into the front family room.

**STEP TWO:**

Spin around seven times, then walk down the stairs.

**STEP THREE:**

Run backwards to the other side of the room.

**STEP FOUR:**

Try and get around Dad and climb under the table.

You get the picture. The boys are laughing at themselves, complaining to Dad, and having a ball. After twenty minutes of treasure hunting they finally reach the elusive "truth treasure box." Little hands open the lid, hoping for a better result this time around. They aren't disappointed. The box contains a nice selection of their favorite candies. Yea Dad!

"Which map was easier to follow?" Dad asks.

"The first one," comes their response.

"Which one was better?"

"The second one. It led to a true treasure," says the oldest.

"That's just like life," Dad shares, "Sometimes it's easier to follow what is false. But it is always better to seek and follow what is true."

They read from Proverbs 2 about the hidden treasure of God's truth and end their time repeating tonight's jingle—"It's best for you to seek what's true." Then they indulge themselves with a mouthful of delicious candy!

# ❧ the power of family nights

The power of family nights is twofold. First, it creates a formal setting within which Dad and Mom can intentionally instill beliefs, values, or character qualities within their child. Rather than defer to the influence of peers and media, or abdicate character training to the school and church, parents create the opportunity to teach their children the things that matter most.

The second impact of family nights is perhaps even more significant than the first. Twenty to sixty minutes of formal fun and instruction can set up countless opportunities for informal reinforcement. These informal impression points do not have to be created, they just happen—at the dinner table, while driving in the car, while watching television, or any other parent/child time together. Once you have formally discussed a given family night topic, you and your children will naturally refer back to those principles during the routine dialogues of everyday life.

If the truth were known, many of us hated family devotions while growing up. We had them sporadically at best, usually whenever our parents were feeling particularly guilty. But that was fine, since the only thing worse was a trip to the dentist. Honestly, do we really think that is what God had in mind when He instructed us to teach our children? As an alternative, many parents are discovering family nights to be a wonderful complement to or replacement for family devotions as a means of passing their beliefs and values to the kids. In fact, many parents hear their kids ask at least three times per week:

*"Can we have family night tonight?"*

Music to Dad's and Mom's ears!

# ⌖ Keys to Effective Family Nights

There are several keys which should be incorporated into effective family nights.

## MAKE IT FUN!

Enjoy yourself, and let the kids have a ball. They may not remember everything you say, but they will always cherish the times of laughter—and so will you.

## KEEP IT SIMPLE!

The minute you become sophisticated or complicated, you've missed the whole point. Don't try to create deeply profound lessons. Just try to reinforce your values and beliefs in a simple, easy-to-understand manner. Read short passages, not long, drawn-out sections of Scripture. Remember: The goal is to keep it simple.

## DON'T DOMINATE!

You want to pull them into the discovery process as much as possible. If you do all the talking, you've missed the mark. Ask questions, give assignments, invite participation in every way possible. They will learn more when you involve all of their senses and emotions.

## GO WITH THE FLOW!

It's fine to start with a well-defined outline, but don't kill spontaneity by becoming overly structured. If an incident or question leads you in a different direction, great! Some of the best impression opportunities are completely unplanned and unexpected.

## MIX IT UP!

Don't allow yourself to get into a rut or routine. Keep the sense of excitement and anticipation through variety. Experiment to discover what works best for your family. Use books, games, videos, props, made-up stories, songs, music or music videos, or even go on a family outing.

## DO IT OFTEN!

We tend to find time for the things that are really important. It is best to set aside one evening per week (the same evening if possible) for family night. Remember, repetition is the best teacher. The more impressions you can create, the more of an impact you will make.

## MAKE A MEMORY!

Find ways to make the lesson stick. For example, just as advertisers create "jingles" to help us remember their products, it is helpful to create family night "jingles" to remember the main theme—such as "It's best for you to seek what's true" or "Just like air, God is there!"

## USE OTHER TOOLS FROM THE HERITAGE BUILDERS TOOL CHEST!

Family night is only one exciting way for you to intentionally build a loving heritage for your family. You'll also want to use these other exciting tools from Heritage Builders.

**The Family Fragrance:** There are five key qualities to a healthy family fragrance, each contributing to an environment of love in the home. It's easy to remember the Fragrance Five by fitting them into an acrostic using the word "Aroma"—

A—Affection
R—Respect
O—Order
M—Merriment
A—Affirmation

**Impression Points:** Ways that we impress on our children our values, preferences, and concerns. We do it through our talk and our actions. We do it intentionally (through such methods as Family Nights), and we do it incidentally.

**The Right Angle:** The Right Angle is the standard of normal healthy living against which our children will be able to measure their atttitudes, actions, and beliefs.

**Traditions:** Meaningful activities which the process of passing on emotional, spiritual, and relational inheritance between generations. Family traditions can play a vital role in this process.

# How to Use This Tool Chest

**Summary page:** For those who like the bottom line, we have provided a summary sheet at the start of each family night session. This abbreviated version of the topic briefly highlights the goal, key Scriptures, activity overview, main points, and life slogan. On the reverse side of this detachable page there is space provided for you to write down any ideas you wish to add or alter as you make the lesson your own.

**Step-by-step:** For those seeking suggestions and directions for each step in the family night process, we have provided a section which walks you through every activity, question, Scripture reading, and discussion point. Feel free to follow each step as written as you conduct the session, or read through this portion in preparation for your time together.

**À la carte:** We strongly encourage you to use the material in this book in an "à la carte" manner. In other words, pick and choose the questions, activities, Scriptures, age-appropriate ideas, etc. which best fit your family. This book is not intended to serve as a curriculum, requiring compliance with our sequence and plan, but rather as a tool chest from which you can grab what works for you and which can be altered to fit your family situation.

**The long and the short of it:** Each family night topic presented in this book includes several activities, related Scriptures, and possible discussion items. Do not feel it is necessary to conduct them all in a single family night. You may wish to spread one topic over several weeks using smaller portions of each chapter, depending upon the attention span of the kids and the energy level of the parents. Remember, short and effective is better than long and thorough.

**Journaling:** Finally, we have provided space with each session for you to capture a record of meaningful comments, funny happenings, and unplanned moments which will inevitably occur during family night. Keep a notebook of these journal entries for future reference. You will treasure this permanent record of the heritage passing process for years to come.

# 1: Sanctity of Human Life Sunday—Made By God

## Understanding the value of human life

**Scripture**
• Psalm 139:13-16; Genesis 9:5-6

| ACTIVITY OVERVIEW | | |
|---|---|---|
| Activity | Summary | Pre-Session Prep |
| Activity 1: Not By Chance | Build a toy using Legos or other blocks, then attempt to build it again by tossing the toys on the ground. | You'll need building block toys such as Legos, K'nex, or Tinkertoys. |
| Activity 2: Defining Worth | Learn the value of life by comparing what's inside a bag to what's inside us. | You'll need paper bags, candies, and a Bible. (Optional: you'll need supplies for making gingerbread cookies.) |

## Main Points:

—God made us!

—We are made in God's image.

**LIFE SLOGAN:** "Knit together by God's hand; each one special in His plan."

*Make it your own*
In the space provided below, outline the flow and add any additional ideas to guide you through the process of conducting this family night.

*Prayer & Praise Items*
In the space provided below, list any items you wish to pray about or give praise for during this family night session.

*Journal*
In the space provided below, capture a record of any fun or meaningful things which happened during this family night session.

## WARM-UP

**Open with Prayer:** Begin by having a family member pray, asking God to help everyone in the family understand more about Him through this time. After prayer, review your last lesson by asking these questions:

- **What did we learn about in our last lesson?**
- **What was the Life Slogan?**
- **Have your actions changed because of what we learned? If so, how?** Encourage family members to give specific examples of how they've applied learning from the past week.

**Share: Today we're going to talk about the most interesting and valuable things God created—us!**

## ACTIVITY 1: Not By Chance

**Point: God made us!**

**Supplies:** You'll need building block toys such as Legos, K'nex, or Tinkertoys.

**Activity:** Gather in a circle on the floor and distribute building toys (such as Legos, K'nex, or Tinkertoys) to each family member. Ask everyone to build a toy. When everyone has finished, ask family members to explain what they built and why. Then explain that you're going to try an experiment and take apart your toy, put it in a box, shake it around, and dump it onto the floor. Express surprise that the building materials didn't re-form your created toy when they landed on the floor. Try the same activity using other family members' toys. After repeating the shaking and tossing activity a few times, consider these questions:

- **How many times would I need to shake the (Legos, K'nex,**

Tinkertoys) before they would fall to the ground in the shape of the toys we originally made? (It wouldn't work; millions of times.)

- Were you surprised that the (Legos, K'nex, Tinkertoys) didn't form our toys when we tossed them on the floor? Why or why not? (No, we made the toys ourselves; no, it takes someone's hands to make those toys.)

**Share: Some people believe that our world—including people—was made by chance. That's kind of like believing that we could toss these building blocks onto the floor and they would form our created toys.**

 Ask:

- What would it take to remake the toys we built at the beginning of this activity? (We'd have to build them from scratch; we'd have to put them together ourselves.)

Have family members attempt to re-create their original toys. Then set these toys in the middle of the circle. Pull off one or two pieces from each toy and set those pieces aside.

 Consider these questions:

- How long will it take for our toys to fix themselves? (It will never work; forever.)
- Why won't the toys fix themselves? (They aren't people; they were created by us; they need someone's help.)

**Share: Tossing blocks onto the floor can't re-create the toys we built. And toys can't fix themselves, either. Building our toys or fixing them when they're broken requires someone with intelligence to do the work. In a similar way, we know that our world—and the people in it—was not created by accident—or by shaking a bunch of parts into the universe—but by someone with intelligence. We know from the Bible that the person who created us is God.**

## Age Adjustments

YOUNGER CHILDREN will appreciate the creativity in God's creation. Take them outdoors (weather permitting) to look at the many different plants, animals, clouds, and other items in nature that God created. To help children understand God's role in creation, use phrases like "God painted the sky" or "God drew the lines on this leaf" as you encounter various aspects of creation. Then go back into your house and marvel together at the wonderful way God made each person in your family. You might remark about your child's eyes, "God made these so we could see," or your child's feet, "God made these so we could walk." End your "time of wonder" by saying something like "Isn't it amazing how good God is at building things!"

# ACTIVITY 2: Defining Worth

**Point: We are made in God's image.**

 **Supplies:** You'll need paper bags, candies, and a Bible. (Optional: You'll need supplies for making gingerbread cookies.)

 **Activity: Read** aloud Genesis 2:7 and Psalm 139:13-16. Then consider these questions:
- **Where did the first human come from?** (God made him; from God.)
- **When does God design us?** (While we're still in the womb; before we're born.)

Take at least four paper bags and put candy in one of them. (You'll want enough bags for each family member to have one, but no fewer than four bags.) Mix up the bags and set them (with the tops folded down) on a table. Then have family members each take one bag at random. Explain that the first bag they touch is the one they must take.

When everyone has a bag, ask them to look inside it. Award one piece of candy from the candy bag to the person who chose that bag. Then collect the bags, reshuffle them, and repeat the activity. Do this three or four times.

 Then consider this question:
- **Which bag were you hoping to get? Why?** (The one with candy because I like candy; the candy one, because it is more valuable.)

**Share: What is inside the bag determines it's value. An empty bag is worth less than a bag filled with candy. In Genesis 9:5-6, we learn that although God created all of the animals, only humans (men and women) were created in God's image. God chose to put the most valuable "stuff" inside us.**

**Ask:**
- **What can we do that animals can't do to show we are made in God's image?** (We have a conscience; we have the ability to love, talk, write, read, choose, etc.)
- **How does it make you feel to know that God made you in**

## Age Adjustments

OLDER CHILDREN AND TEENAGERS probably will face or have faced the "Creation vs. Evolution" discussion at school. Use this family night as a springboard into discussion with your older children and teenagers about God's role in creation. Be sensitive to the confusion they might have regarding this issue. If you're unsure how to answer their questions, make a commitment together to do some research and find biblically based answers during the next week. Help children know that it's okay not to know all of the details of creation, but that it's ultimately important to know that there is indeed a Creator, and that He created us in His image.

His image? (I feel special; it makes me happy; it makes me feel closer to God.)

• **If we're made in God's image, how should we care for our bodies?** (We should not hurt other people; we should eat good foods; we should respect each other.)

If you have time (and the necessary supplies), mix up some gingerbread cookie dough and make some gingerbread men (and women, if you have the right cookie cutters). After baking the cookies, enjoy decorating them. Point out that just like these cookies are made in our image, we're made in the image of God. Then enjoy the cookies together.

 **WRAP-UP**

Gather everyone in a circle and have family members take turns answering this question: **What's one thing you've learned about God today?**

Next, tell kids you've got a new "Life Slogan" you'd like to share with them.

**Life slogan: Today's Life Slogan is this: "Knit together by God's hand; each one special in His plan."** Have family members repeat the slogan two or three times to help them learn it. Then encourage them to practice saying it during the week so they can talk about it at your next family night session.

**Close in Prayer:** Allow time for each family member to share prayer concerns and answers to prayer. Then close your time together with prayer for each concern. Thank God for listening to and caring about us.

Remember to record your prayer requests so you can refer to them in the future as you see God answering them.

## Additional Resources:

*Spinning Worlds, Volcanoes and Earthquakes, Lightning and Rainbows, Oceans and Rivers,* all by Michael Carroll (ages 8-12)

*The Children's Discovery Bible* by Charlene Heibert (ages 4-7)

*The Picture Bible* by Iva Hoth (ages 8-12)

*The Baby Bible Storybook* by Robin Currie (ages 0-3)

*Pocket Bible Stories: The World God Made* (ages 4-7)

Dinosaurs and the Creation Story CD-ROM (ages 6-11)

*Pencil Fun Books: Adam and Eve* (ages 4-7)

# 2: Valentine's Day— What Love Is

## Understanding the true meaning of Christian love

**Scripture**
• 1 Corinthians 13

| ACTIVITY OVERVIEW | | |
| --- | --- | --- |
| Activity | Summary | Pre-Session Prep |
| Activity 1: Focusing on Others | Play mirror games and learn how love focuses on others | You'll need a snack and a Bible. |
| Activity 2: Love Cards | Create Valentine's Day cards for family members, friends, and Jesus. | You'll need colored paper, markers, crayons, scissors, tape or glue, and a Bible |

## Main Points:

—Love is unselfish—it focuses on others.

—God teaches us about love through His Son, our families, and friends.

**LIFE SLOGAN:** "Unselfish love is from above."

### Make it your own

*In the space provided below, outline the flow and add any additional ideas to guide you through the process of conducting this family night.*

### Prayer & Praise Items

*In the space provided below, list any items you wish to pray about or give praise for during this family night session.*

### Journal

*In the space provided below, capture a record of any fun or meaningful things which happened during this family night session.*

## WARM-UP

**Open with Prayer:** Begin by having a family member pray, asking God to help everyone in the family understand more about Him through this time. After prayer, review your last lesson by asking these questions:

- **What did we learn about in our last lesson?**
- **What was the Life Slogan?**
- **Have your actions changed because of what we learned? If so, how?** Encourage family members to give specific examples of how they've applied learning from the past week.

**Share:** Valentine's Day is a time when people say "I love you" to each other. We're going to learn all about the kind of love Christians share with others—and then we're going to create special cards to share that love with others.

## ACTIVITY 1: Focusing on Others

**Point: Love is unselfish—it focuses on others.**

**Supplies:** You'll need a snack and a Bible.

**Activity:** Have family members take turns "mirroring" each other. Have one person sit or stand directly across from another and copy that person's expressions and actions. Encourage family members to do creative actions and expressions. After a few minutes for this activity, consider these questions:

- **What was necessary for doing this activity well?** (We had to focus on our partner; we had to concentrate.)
- **How is this activity like love?** (It focuses on other people; we do things others are doing rather than just what we want to do.)

**Read** 1 Corinthians 13. **Then share: When we think of the word "love," lots of things come to mind. You may say that you love**

ice cream, or that you love a particular television show. But we're going to talk about the kind of love that God has for us—and how we can share that same kind of love with others. It all begins by doing what we did in this activity—focusing on others rather than ourselves.

Set your snack foods on a table. Then instruct family members that they cannot eat the snack themselves, but that they must feed someone else the snack. This can be fun as well as a challenge for younger children. After family members have enjoyed a snack, form a circle and consider these questions:

- **What was it like to not get to eat a snack by yourself?** (I really wanted one; I was glad someone else fed me; it was hard to wait.)
- **How would you have felt if you fed someone else, but no one fed you?** (I'd have been sad; it would be okay, I was glad to share the snack with Mom.)

## Age Adjustments

OLDER CHILDREN AND TEENAGERS will benefit from exploring a few other verses that talk about love. Consider these verses for discussion: Matthew 19:19 (Love your neighbor as yourself); Mark 12:30 (Love the Lord God with all your heart, with all your soul, with all your mind, and with all your strength); John 13:34 (Love one another); Ephesians 5:25 (Love your wife); 1 Peter 2:17 (Love the brotherhood of believers); Matthew 5:44 (Love your enemies). Use these verses to spark discussion on how the love expressed in the Bible compares to the love expressed in popular media such as television, movies, and music.

**Share:** In 1 Corinthians 13, we are given a definition of what true Christian love is all about. One of the characteristics of love is that it isn't self-seeking. That means it isn't selfish. True Christian love is expressed without expecting anything in return. That would be like feeding the delicious snack to someone else but not expecting to have any yourself. That's not an easy thing to do.

Have family members think of times they have said things such as "If you [perform some action], I'll give you a kiss (or a hug)." **Then share: When we ask for something in trade for our love, that's called conditional love. Conditional love is the kind of love that says: "I'll love if you if you get me some ice cream." But the Bible tells us that the best kind of love is unconditional. That's what we might call "just because" love. God tells us that He loves us—not that we have to do certain things to get His love.** It's always there for us to have.

## ACTIVITY 2: Love Cards

**Point: God teaches us about love through His Son, our families, and friends.**

**Supplies:** You'll need colored paper, markers, crayons, scissors, tape or glue, and a Bible.

**Activity:** Ask children to tell you where they learn about love. Some answers might be: from God; from parents; from watching television; from books; from the Bible. Then go around and give each family member a great big hug.

 Consider these questions:
- **What did I just do?** (Give a hug; show love.)
- **What are other ways people show you love?** (By reading a bedtime story; by caring for me; by playing with me.)
- **Who are some other people who show you love?** (Teachers; friends; our pastor; neighbors.)

**Share:** We learn about love from family members and friends who love us. We also learn about love from the story of Jesus in the Bible. On Valentine's Day, we usually send cards to people we care about. Let's do something a little different today. We're going to create three large Valentine's Day cards for people who have taught us about love. Of course, we also love these people, so it's a good idea to make cards for them.

Help your family members create three big Valentine's Day cards: one for family members (include as many relatives as you can); one for friends (from school, church, work); and one for Jesus. **Reread** 1 Corinthians 13 as you work together on the cards. When the cards are complete, have each family member use an ink pad and mark a thumb print on each of the three cards.

**Share:** These thumb prints represent the imprint that our families, friends, and most importantly, Jesus, have had in our lives and in our understanding of love.

When the cards are complete, place them on a table or tape them up on a wall for all to see. Ask kids to think about where they've learned about love each time they see the cards, and to say a little prayer thanking God for giving us the picture of love in Jesus' life.

## WRAP-UP

Gather everyone in a circle and have family members take turns answering this question: **What's one thing you've learned about God today?**

Next, tell kids you've got a new "Life Slogan" you'd like to share with them.

**Life slogan: Today's Life Slogan is this: "Unselfish love is from above."** Have family members repeat the slogan two or three times to help them learn it. Then encourage them to practice saying it during the week so they can talk about it at your next family night session.

**Close in Prayer:** Allow time for each family member to share prayer concerns and answers to prayer. Then close your time together with prayer for each concern. Thank God for listening to and caring about us.

Remember to record your prayer requests so you can refer to them in the future as you see God answering them.

### Additional Resources:

*Jesus Loves Me, Jesus Loves the Little Children, Jesus Is with Me,* all by Debby Anderson (ages 0-3)
*Psalms for a Child's Heart* by Sheryl Crawford (ages 4-7)
*Adam Raccoon and the King's Big Dinner* by Glen Keane (ages 4-7)

# 3: Easter—God's Plans

## Exploring how Jesus' death was God's plan to save us

### Scripture
• John 3:16; Romans 3:23; Romans 6:23; Colossians 2:13-14
• Hebrews 12:1; 1 John 1:9

| ACTIVITY OVERVIEW | | |
|---|---|---|
| Activity | Summary | Pre-Session Prep |
| Activity 1: God's Plans | Make plans and discuss God's plan for Jesus | You'll need paper and pencils or pens, materials to make a large cross (wood, hammer, nails), and a Bible. |
| Activity 2: Confession | Play games and learn how confession allows Jesus to forgive us and "clean our slates." | You'll need a magic slate, candies (such as M&Ms), paper, pencils, bathrobe ties or soft rope, items that can used to weigh someone down, and a Bible. |

## Main Points:

—Easter was God's plan for Jesus.

—If we confess our sins, Jesus will forgive us and cleanse our hearts.

**LIFE SLOGAN:** "Jesus' death is the key, to unlock God's plan for me."

### Make it your own

*In the space provided below, outline the flow and add any additional ideas to guide you through the process of conducting this family night.*

### Prayer & Praise Items

*In the space provided below, list any items you wish to pray about or give praise for during this family night session.*

### Journal

*In the space provided below, capture a record of any fun or meaningful things which happened during this family night session.*

We intentionally have provided more material than we would expect to be used in a single "Family Night" session. You know your family's unique interests and life circumstances best, so feel free to adapt this lesson to meet your family members' needs. Remember, short and simple is better than long and comprehensive.

## WARM-UP

**Open with Prayer:** Begin by having a family member pray, asking God to help everyone in the family understand more about Him through this time. After prayer, review your last lesson by asking these questions:

- **What did we learn about in our last lesson?**
- **What was the Life Slogan?**
- **Have your actions changed because of what we learned? If so, how?** Encourage family members to give specific examples of how they've applied learning from the past week.

**Share: Today we're going to talk about how Jesus' death was God's plan to save us and that if we confess our sins, Jesus will forgive us and cleanse us.**

## ACTIVITY 1: God's Plan

**Point: Easter was God's plan for Jesus.**

**Supplies:** You'll need paper and pencils or pens, materials to make a large cross (wood, hammer, nails), and a Bible.

**Activity:** Ask your children to describe what a "plan" is and how one is made. Here are some responses kids might give:

- A plan is something for the future.
- A plan is something you do when you're getting ready to do something.

## Age Adjustments

YOUNGER CHILDREN may have some difficulty understanding why they're nailing papers to the cross. You may want to have them draw mean faces on their papers and pretend that those faces are all the mean things they do. Then tell children that Jesus died on the cross so we could get rid of all the mean things we do and have a happy life with Him. While this may be a simplistic picture of salvation, it can help prepare younger hearts and minds for the true meaning of the cross for a time when they're old enough to better understand it.

FOR OLDER CHILDREN AND TEENAGERS, it may be good to have them read a few passages which show that the Crucifixion was revealed as God's plan hundreds of years before Jesus was born. Have them read Psalm 22, regarded by many Bible scholars as a prophetic passage describing the Crucifixion. Compare it to the Gospel passages (Matthew, Mark, Luke, and John) describing the death of Christ. We also see that Jesus' death was God's plan when we read about the Passover in Exodus 12. Discuss how the Passover is like the sacrifice of Jesus.

• A plan is a list of things you need to do.

• A plan is like a recipe.

After helping to clarify what a plan is, ask family members to think of some event you should plan for. This could be everything from a spring or summer trip to a birthday party to a visit to the grocery store.

With your family's help, make a plan for that event, listing your ideas on the paper.

 Then **read** aloud John 3:16. Consider these questions:

- **What does this Bible passage tell us about God's plan for Jesus?** (God planned to send Jesus to die on the cross.)
- **What does this Bible passage tell us about God's plan for us?** (God wanted to save us; God loves us; God wants us to live forever.)

Discuss how God made a plan to save us and to make us His sons and daughters. Explain how God planned for Jesus to come, die on the cross, and be raised from the dead.

 **Read** or summarize Romans 3:23 and 6:23. Explain that those who sin against God will be separated from God forever. Then **read** or summarize Colossians 2:13-14. Explain how God takes our sins and nails them to the cross. Have your family members help you to create a wooden cross. You can do this by cutting a single 2x4x8 into five-foot and three-foot lengths, then nailing them together to form a cross.

Have family members each write their name on a sheet of paper along with the word "Sins." Then nail the papers to the cross. You may need to help younger children with this activity.

**Share: When Jesus died on the cross, He took all of our sins with Him. Because of this we get to be a part of God's family.**

## ACTIVITY 2: Confession

**Point: If we confess our sins, Jesus will forgive us and cleanse our hearts.**

**Supplies:** You'll need a magic slate, candies (such as M&Ms), paper, pencils, bathrobe ties or soft rope, items that can be used to weigh someone down, and a Bible.

**Activity:** Announce to your family that you're going to have a fun time playing games. Then take out the magic slate (you may want more than one if you have more than one child). Take turns playing tictacktoe using the slate. Award two candies to each winner and one to each loser. Point out how you can clear the slate by just lifting the front plastic sheet.

NOTE: If you can't find a magic slate, use a small blackboard and chalk or a reuseable noteboard that can be wiped clean with a cloth.

After you've played a few games of tictacktoe, give a family member the magic slate and whisper to him or her the name of an animal. Have that person draw the animal while other family members attempt to guess it. Repeat this activity until each family member has had at least one turn. Don't forget to clear the magic slate after each turn!

When you're finished with the animal drawing game, take the magic slate and write on it something you've done wrong, then hold it in front of you. For example, you might write "I yelled when I was angry." Then have family members entangle you with a bathrobe tie or soft rope and give you something heavy to hold (such as a big book). Attempt to walk around the room. Then add another item to the slate or simply tell family members about another time you did or said something wrong. Once again, have family members wrap you with more bathrobe ties or soft rope and give you another heavy item. Repeat one or more times, with family members adding more ropes or heavy items each time. Explain how Hebrews 12:1 says that sin (or things we do that are wrong) entangles us and weighs us down, just like the ropes and heavy objects. Then have someone **read** aloud 1 John 1:9 and explain that when we confess (or tell Jesus about) our sins, Jesus will forgive us and clean our hearts up. Go ahead and ask Jesus for forgiveness for the things on the magic slate, then have someone lift the plastic sheet to make them disappear. Also, have family members help you remove the ties and weights.

If appropriate, repeat this activity with each family member taking a turn being entangled by sin.

 After everyone's had a turn, form a circle and discuss these questions:

- **What did it feel like to be tied up and weighed down?**
(I couldn't move; I didn't like it; I thought it was fun at first, but then it wasn't.)

- **How is that like what it feels like after you've sinned or done something wrong?**
(It's the same—I don't like it; when we do something wrong sometimes it seems fun at first, but then it isn't.)

**Share:** When we sin against God, we get all tangled up. But because God sent His son to die on the cross, we can ask Him to untangle us and forgive us for the wrong things we say and do. If we confess our sins, Jesus will erase the mess and make us clean again!

### WRAP-UP

Gather everyone in a circle and have family members take turns answering this question: **What's one thing you've learned about God today?**

Next, tell kids you've got a new "Life Slogan" you'd like to share with them.

**Life slogan:** Today's Life Slogan is this: "Jesus' death is the key, to unlock God's plan for me." Have family members repeat the slogan two or three times to help them learn it. Then encourage them to practice saying it during the week so they can talk about it at your next family night session.

**Close in Prayer:** Allow time for each family member to share prayer concerns and answers to prayer. Then close your time together with prayer for each concern. Thank God for listening to and caring about us.

Remember to record your prayer requests so you can refer to them in the future as you see God answering them.

**Additional Resources:**

See page 38.

## Age Adjustments

FOR OLDER CHILDREN AND TEENAGERS, go deeper with your discussion about sin and the importance of confession. Explore together how our society encourages behaviors that are sinful and how difficult it is to make the right choices in life. Ask older children and teenagers to share the temptations they face at school and among peers. Then encourage your children to spend time in prayer each morning before school asking God to help them make good choices and asking God to use them to reach out to those at school who don't yet know Jesus.

# 4: Easter—Impressions

## Exploring Jesus' death and resurrection

### Scripture
• Selected passages from the Gospel account of Easter

| ACTIVITY OVERVIEW | | |
|---|---|---|
| **Activity** | **Summary** | **Pre-Session Prep** |
| Activity 1: From Sadness . . . | Think about sad things, then begin an egg hunt to learn about Jesus' death. | You'll need a variety of supplies (see the first activity for specific preparation tips), and a Bible. |
| Activity 2: . . . To Joy | Continue the egg hunt and learn about the joy of Jesus' resurrection. | You'll need a variety of supplies (see the first activity for specific preparation tips), and a Bible. |

## Main Points:

— Jesus died for our sins.

— Jesus was victorious over death and sin.

**LIFE SLOGAN:** "At Easter time, it is Christ we find."

### Make it your own

*In the space provided below, outline the flow and add any additional ideas to guide you through the process of conducting this family night.*

### Prayer & Praise Items

*In the space provided below, list any items you wish to pray about or give praise for during this family night session.*

### Journal

*In the space provided below, capture a record of any fun or meaningful things which happened during this family night session.*

## WARM-UP

**Open with Prayer:** Begin by having a family member pray, asking God to help everyone in the family understand more about Him through this time. After prayer, review your last lesson by asking these questions:

- **What did we learn about in our last lesson?**
- **What was the Life Slogan?**
- **Have your actions changed because of what we learned? If so, how?** Encourage family members to give specific examples of how they've applied learning from the past week.

**Share: Today we're going to talk about how Jesus' death was God's plan to save us and that if we confess our sins, Jesus will forgive us and cleanse us.**

## ACTIVITY 1: From Sadness...

**Point: Jesus died for our sins.**

**Supplies:** You'll need 12 plastic eggs. Label the eggs 1 to 12, then place a slip of paper listing the following Scripture reference in each appropriate egg.

Egg #1—Luke 22:1-6; Egg #2—Mark 14:12-26;
Egg #3—Luke 22:47-54; Egg #4—Luke 22:55-62;
Egg #5—Matthew 27:1-10; Egg #6—Matthew 27:11-31;
Egg #7—Luke 23:26-34; Egg #8—Luke 23:35-43; Egg #9—Luke 23:44-53; Egg #10—Matthew 27:59-61; Egg #11—Luke 23:54–24:1; Egg #12—nothing.

Optionally, you can add the following items to the appropriate number eggs: Egg #1—a toy lamb or a picture of a lamb; Egg #2—a small piece of bread; Egg #3—nickels; Egg #4—picture of a rooster; Egg #5—piece of purple cloth; Egg #6—thorns (from a rose bush or other plant); Egg #7—a tiny cross (you can

make one out of matchsticks); Egg #8—a small sponge; Egg #9—a nail; Egg #10—a rock; Egg #11—some spices; Egg #12—nothing.

NOTE: For a "prepackaged" way to do this activity, look for "Resurrection Eggs" from Family Life Ministries at your local Christian bookstore.

**Activity:** Hide the plastic eggs around your house. During this activity, you'll be searching for the first 7 eggs and discussing the contents of the eggs. **Share: Today we're going to explore the real meaning of Jesus' death and resurrection. In both of our activities, we're going to go on an egg hunt and find clues about the sadness of Jesus' death—and the joy of His resurrection.**

Send children out to find the eggs in numbered order. Then follow the instructions below for each egg.

When Egg #1 is found, dump it out and **read** Luke 22:1-6. **Then share: The Passover was a celebration of the Exodus (or escape) from Egypt. Just before they were allowed to leave Egypt, the Israelites painted lamb's blood on their doorframes to save their firstborn sons from death. The sacrifice of these lambs is similar to the way Jesus became our "sacrificial lamb" when He spilled His blood on the cross. Christ became our Passover (or our Savior from death).**

When Egg #2 is found, dump it out and **read** Mark 14:12-26. **Then share: The Passover meal included lamb, unleavened bread (flat bread that has no yeast), sauces, and other ceremonial drinks.**

Enjoy a brief snack time with your family. Crackers and juice make a great snack and help children better understand the Passover meal.

When Egg #3 is found, dump it out and **read** Luke 22:47-54. Consider these questions:
- **Why did Judas kiss Jesus?** (To point Him out to the Roman soldiers.)
- **When we kiss someone, it's usually because we love them. But Judas' kiss had no meaning. When do we do things like this that have no meaning?** (When we say we care about someone, but don't show it; when we say we love God, but don't show it.)

When Egg #4 is found, dump it out and **read** Luke 22:55-62. **Then share: Peter denied Christ, just as we sometimes do. But** after he denied Christ, Peter realized what he had done. God was able to use him for greater works.

 Ask:
- **How are we like Peter?** (We make mistakes; God can use us even though we mess up.)

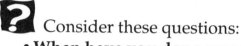 When Egg #5 is found, dump it out and **read** Matthew 27:1-10. **Share: Judas realized he'd done something wrong and felt guilty. That's why he threw away the coins.**

Consider these questions:
- **When have you done something wrong that you later felt guilty for?** (When I lied to Mom; when I took a toy from a friend; when I broke a vase.)
- **How can we fix these wrong things?** (Say we're sorry; give back the toy; pay for the broken vase.)

**Share: When we've done something wrong, like lied to Mom, we need to ask forgiveness for our wrong choice. That doesn't take away the lie, but it does give us a clean start to do things right next time.**

When Egg #6 is found, dump it out and **read** Matthew 27:11-31. Have family members spend a time in silence, thinking about the awful experience Jesus must have had as described in this passage. **Then share: Jesus had done nothing wrong, but people yelled at him, made fun of Him, and beat Him. Even though He wasn't deserving of death, He chose to go to the cross for us.**

When Egg #7 is found, dump it out and **read** Luke 23:26-34.

 Consider these questions:
- **If Jesus was truly God, why didn't He call for angels to save Him from the pain of the cross?** (Because He was sup-

## Age Adjustments

OLDER CHILDREN AND TEENAGERS **may enjoy learning about the origin of some of our Easter traditions. Here is a brief summary to spark discussion. This information comes from Panati's** *Extraordinary Origins of Everyday Things.*

*Why rabbits?* **In the second century when the missionaries were spreading out around Rome, they encountered numerous pagan holidays. In an effort to minimize or eliminate any persecution, they would try to celebrate religious holidays when the pagan celebrated a nonreligious holiday. For Easter, they discoverd that the pagans held a festival honoring the goddess of spring and off-spring named Eastre. This goddess was worshiped through her earthly symbol, the rabbit.**

*What about the egg?* **Over the years, the egg has represented birth and resurrection. Egyptians buried them in tombs. Greeks placed them on their graves. Eggs were given as gifts. Wealthy people would coat the eggs with gold. So when the church went looking for a symbol, the egg was a natural fit for the birth and resurrection of Christ.**

posed to die for us; because He wouldn't have died for our sins; because He was also a man.)

- **What does it feel like to imagine Jesus dying on the cross?** (Sad; it makes me feel like crying; scared.)

**Share: When Jesus died on the cross, it was a sad day indeed for His followers. But we know something now that they didn't know until a few days later—that Jesus would rise from the dead.**

## ACTIVITY 2:....To Joy

**Point: Jesus was victorious over death and sin.**

 **Supplies:** See the first activity for supplies and set-up.

**Share: We've looked at all of the sad things about Easter—now let's look at the joy-filled parts of the Easter story.**

Have children continue their egg hunt.

When Egg #8 is found, dump it out and **read** Luke 23:35-43. **Then share: In the middle of his pain, the man next to Jesus realized his need for forgiveness. What a joy that must have been to know that he would be with Christ after death!**

 Ask:

- **How do you think Jesus felt when the man next to Him asked to be remembered?** (Happy; relieved; joyful.)
- **The man who Jesus said would be with Him in paradise probably had done many bad things. Why was he going to be with Jesus?** (Because he accepted Christ; because he realized his mistakes and wanted to change.)

**Share: This passage reminds us that it's not the things we do that get us into heaven, but it's our faith in God that grants us eternal life.**

When Egg #9 is found, dump it out and **read** Luke 23:44-53. **Share: When Jesus cried out "Father, I Give you My life," He breathed His last breath. While this may seem to be a sad event, it is also a joyful one, for Jesus had died in place of us. We have all done many things wrong—we've sinned against God. But only Jesus, who had no sin, could die in our place.**

Spend a moment in prayer, thanking God for sending Jesus to die in our place and remove the barriers between us and God.

When Egg #10 is found, dump it out and **read** Matthew 27:59-61. Have family members climb under a blanket or other cover. While there, discuss the following questions:

• **What does it feel like to be in the dark?** (Scary; it makes me sad; sometimes I'm afraid.)

**Share:** When we think about Jesus' body being placed into a dark tomb, we might feel scared or sad too. A big rock was rolled in front of the tomb to keep it sealed tight.

Send a family member out to find Egg #11. When he or she returns, dump out the egg and **read** aloud Luke 23:54–24:1. Ask:

• **In what ways were the women obedient to God?** (They stayed with Jesus; they came to care for His body.)

**Share:** Even though their actions seemed small, these women did all they could to show their love for Jesus. Because of their devotion, they were also the first to see Him alive.

While still under the blanket, send someone out to collect Egg #12. When you open it, shout "It's empty!" and toss off the blanket. **Read** aloud Luke 24:1-12 and ask:

• **What does it feel like to know that Jesus rose from the dead?** (Exciting; it makes me happy.)
• **What feelings do you have about Easter now?** (Happiness, because Jesus rose from the dead; sadness, because the people were mean to Jesus.)

**Share:** Just as our final egg was empty, so was the tomb when the women went to prepare Jesus' body. Easter is a time of many emotions—but ultimately of joy because our Savior not only rose from the dead—He lives today.

## WRAP-UP

Gather everyone in a circle and have family members take turns answering this question: **What's one thing you've learned about God today?**

Next, tell kids you've got a new "Life Slogan" you'd like to share with them.

**Life slogan:** Today's Life Slogan is this: **"At Easter time, it is Christ we find."** Have family members repeat the slogan two or three times to

help them learn it. Then encourage them to practice saying it during the week so they can talk about it at your next family night session.

**Close in Prayer:** Allow time for each family member to share prayer concerns and answers to prayer. Then close your time together with prayer for each concern. Thank God for listening to and caring about us.

Remember to record your prayer requests so you can refer to them in the future as you see God answering them.

## Additional Resources:

*My Lord, My God* by Calvin Miller (family reading)
*The Children's Discovery Bible* by Charlene Heibert (ages 4-7)
*The Picture Bible* by Iva Hoth (ages 8-12)
*Kids-Life Easter Storybook* by Mary Hollingsworth (ages 4-7)
*Pencil Fun Books: Jesus Lives* (ages 4-7)
*The Tale of Three Trees* by Angela Elwell Hunt (ages 4 and up)
*Sad News, Glad News* by Lois Rock (ages 4-8)
*Little Rose of Sharon* by Nan Gurley (ages 4-8)
Easter Celebration Kit (egg decorating family activity/ages 5 and up)

# 5: Mother's Day—Honoring Mom

## Celebrating the importance of Moms

### Scripture
- Proverbs 24:3-4
- 2 Timothy 1:4-7

| ACTIVITY OVERVIEW | | |
|---|---|---|
| Activity | Summary | Pre-Session Prep |
| Activity 1: Center Stage | Give Mom a special seat and shower her with praise and party favors. | You'll need confetti and streamers, a comfortable chair, a wash basin with warm water, two cloths, and a Bible. |
| Activity 2: A Servant's Heart | Serve one another and learn about the importance of Mom's servant attitude. | You'll need a variety of objects depending on the activity chosen (see lesson), and you'll need a Bible. |

## Main Points:

—Moms are special and important to us and to God.

—Moms model Jesus' love when they serve gladly.

**LIFE SLOGAN:** "Mom's loving heart is our favorite part."

*Make it your own*
In the space provided below, outline the flow and add any additional ideas to guide you through the process of conducting this family night.

*Prayer & Praise Items*
In the space provided below, list any items you wish to pray about or give praise for during this family night session.

*Journal*
In the space provided below, capture a record of any fun or meaningful things which happened during this family night session.

## WARM-UP

**Open with Prayer:** Begin by having a family member pray, asking God to help everyone in the family understand more about Him through this time. After prayer, review your last lesson by asking these questions:

- **What did we learn about in our last lesson?**
- **What was the Life Slogan?**
- **Have your actions changed because of what we learned? If so, how?** Encourage family members to give specific examples of how they've applied learning from the past week.

**Share: Mother's Day is a special day because it helps us remember the important role that Mom plays in our lives. Today we're going to celebrate Mom and think about ways Mom models Jesus' love.**

## ACTIVITY 1: Center Stage

**Point: Moms are special and important to us and to God.**

 **Supplies:** You'll need confetti and streamers, a comfortable chair, a wash basin with warm water, two cloths, and a Bible.

**Activity:** Place your most comfortable chair in the center of the room. Have Mom sit in the chair. Then join children in tossing confetti and streamers as you dance around the chair singing "We Love Mom" to any tune that comes to mind.

After celebrating Mom with your song and party favors, have family members take turns listing all the things Mom does for the family. This could be everything from washing the dishes, to taking the kids to school, to working at an office to help support the family. Have each person say at least three things they appreciate about what Mom does.

Then have children list things that Mom does exclusively for herself. This could include hobbies, reading, taking a bath, and so on.

 Ask:

- **What did you notice about the lists?** (Mom does more for us than for herself; Mom does a lot for us; Mom has lots of interests.)

**Read** aloud Proverbs 24:3-4. Then ask:

- **What are ways your mom is wise?** (She knows how to help with math; she knows how to make great cookies; she knows when I need a hug.)

**Share: In honor of all that Mom does for us, and all the wisdom she brings to our home, let's serve her in a special way.**

Get out the wash basin and help your children wash Mom's feet. This can be a joyful time or a more serious time—either is okay. As you wash Mom's feet, share with your children how Jesus washed His disciples' feet. Then help children dry Mom's feet and give her a big hug.

## Age Adjustments

YOUNGER CHILDREN may laugh or giggle during the feet-washing experience. That's normal since this activity is so out of the ordinary. Acknowledge their discomfort, but urge them to truly serve Mom during this time. (There's nothing better than a great foot rub after a long day.) You can help younger children understand the importance of this experience by showing them a picture of Jesus washing the disciples' feet from a children's Bible.

FOR OLDER CHILDREN AND TEENAGERS, it may be fun to select a special song to perform for Mom as a lip sync show. Perhaps "How Sweet It Is to Be Loved by You" by James Taylor or "I L.O.V.E. You" by Take Six. The whole family will laugh and have fun together making fools of themselves to show Mom how much they love her!

## ACTIVITY 2: A Servant's Heart

**Point: Moms model Jesus' love when they serve gladly.**

 **Supplies:** You'll need a variety of objects depending on the activity chosen (see lesson), and you'll need a Bible.

**Share: When Mom does nice things for us, she is modeling Jesus' love. But since this is Mother's Day, we're going to model Jesus' love to her.**

Spend a few minutes with your children brainstorming ideas of how they can show love to Mom. Here are a few examples to consider:

- Cook supper
- Give a backrub
- Clean up the kitchen or another room
- Do the laundry

- Dust the furniture
- Prepare a bubble bath with candles and a comfortable tub pillow
- Make cookies

Encourage family members to come up with as long a list as possible. Then hand that list to Mom and ask her to mark the two or three things she'd love most to have the rest of the family do. Then, if time and supplies allow, help your children to serve Mom by doing these activities.

 After Mom has been served in your chosen ways, **read** aloud 2 Timothy 1:4-7. **Then share: Moms are special because they model Jesus' love by serving and making wise decisions. And they're also important because they pass down their faith to their children, just as described in this passage.**

To end your family night celebrating Mom, have children each choose one way they'll show their appreciation to Mom each day for the next seven days. For example, one child might choose to give five hugs a day while another might offer to set the table for dinner. Continue to reinforce the value of Mom's role throughout the coming year so Mother's Day doesn't stand out as the only day each year when Mom feels special. Help your family learn to celebrate each others' roles throughout the year.

## WRAP-UP

Gather everyone in a circle and have family members take turns answering this question: **What's one thing you've learned about God today?**

Next, tell kids you've got a new "Life Slogan" you'd like to share with them.

**Life slogan: Today's Life Slogan is this: "Mom's loving heart is our favorite part."** Have family members repeat the slogan two or three times to help them learn it. Then encourage them to practice saying it during the week so they can talk about it at your next family night session.

### Age Adjustments

FOR OLDER CHILDREN AND TEENAGERS, Mom's role may include lots of transporting to and from school, baseball games, band practices, friends' houses, and dozens of other locations. Have children make a list of all the places Mom has taken them during the past few weeks or months. Then have children think of one nice thing they can do for Mom for each of the locations on the list. Help children make plans to do those nice things in the coming weeks.

**Close in Prayer:** Allow time for each family member to share prayer concerns and answers to prayer. Then close your time together with prayer for each concern. Thank God for listening to and caring about us.

Remember to record your prayer requests so you can refer to them in the future as you see God answering them.

## Additional Resources:

*My Son, My Savior* by Calvin Miller (family reading)
*The Children's Discovery Bible* by Charlene Heibert (ages 4-7)
*Little Rose of Sharon* by Nan Gurley (ages 4-8)

# 6: Father's Day/Mother's Day—A Picture of God

## Exploring how God created dads and moms in His image

*Note: This family night can be used for either Father's Day or Mother's Day. Adjust as appropriate throughout the activities.*

### Scripture
• Genesis 1:26-27

| ACTIVITY OVERVIEW | | |
|---|---|---|
| Activity | Summary | Pre-Session Prep |
| Activity 1: An Image | Make shadow portraits and learn about images. | You'll need large sheets of paper, pencils, a bright light, a picture of your family, and a Bible. |
| Activity 2: God Is Like a Great Dad (or Mom) | Compare some of the attributes of a dad or mom to God's attributes. | You'll need supplies to make a collage (magazines, paper, tape or glue, scissors). |

## Main Points:

—God chose to make dads (or moms) as a picture of Himself.

—We can learn about God from Dad (or Mom).

**LIFE SLOGAN:** "To understand His love, God gave a father's (or mother's) love."

### Make it your own

*In the space provided below, outline the flow and add any additional ideas to guide you through the process of conducting this family night.*

### Prayer & Praise Items

*In the space provided below, list any items you wish to pray about or give praise for during this family night session.*

### Journal

*In the space provided below, capture a record of any fun or meaningful things which happened during this family night session.*

## Session Tip

We intentionally have provided more material than we would expect to be used in a single "Family Night" session. You know your family's unique interests and life circumstances best, so feel free to adapt this lesson to meet your family members' needs. Remember, short and simple is better than long and comprehensive.

## WARM-UP

**Open with Prayer:** Begin by having a family member pray, asking God to help everyone in the family understand more about Him through this time. After prayer, review your last lesson by asking these questions:

- **What did we learn about in our last lesson?**
- **What was the Life Slogan?**
- **Have your actions changed because of what we learned? If so, how?** Encourage family members to give specific examples of how they've applied learning from the past week.

**Share: Today we're going to learn about a great idea God had—to give us a dad (or a mom). We're also going to explore how God teaches us about Himself through our earthly father (or mother).**

## ACTIVITY 1: An Image

**Point: God chose to make dads (or moms) as a picture of Himself.**

**Supplies:** You'll need large sheets of paper, pencils, a bright light, a picture of your family, and a Bible.

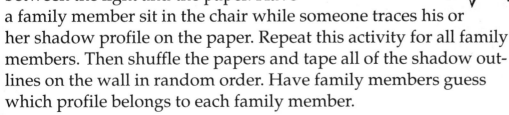

**Activity:** Set up a bright lamp near a flat, blank wall. Carefully tape a large sheet of paper or newsprint on the wall. Place a chair sideways between the light and the paper. Have a family member sit in the chair while someone traces his or her shadow profile on the paper. Repeat this activity for all family members. Then shuffle the papers and tape all of the shadow outlines on the wall in random order. Have family members guess which profile belongs to each family member.

Consider these questions:
- **How can you identify the shadow portraits?** (I recognize the shape of the nose; I can tell by the size of the head; it looks just like the person.)
- **How are these portraits "images" of us?** (They show what we look like; they're drawings of us; we can tell who they are by looking at them.)

 Pass around a picture of your family and discuss this question:
- **Is this our family? Why or why not?** (Yes, we are the people in the picture; no, it's a picture of our family.)

Hold up the picture and **share: This is not our family, but a picture of our family. We take pictures to send to other people so they know what we look like. A picture could also be called an image. An image is something that we can identify because it looks like something or someone we know.**

**Read** aloud Genesis 1:26-27. Explain that moms (or dads) are God's idea.

Consider this question:
- **Why do you think God made dads (or moms)?** (Because He knew we'd need them; because He wanted us to see an image of Him; because He loves us.)

## Age Adjustments

OLDER CHILDREN AND TEENAGERS may enjoy a variation on the shadow portrait activity. Have them each trace a hand, elbow, knee, and foot, each on a separate sheet of paper (marking the back of the papers with their initials). Then collect the papers and have a contest to see who is the fastest at matching the traced body parts to the person. Award a fun prize to the person with the fastest time. Then launch into the discussion about image—and what it means that dads or moms are created in God's image.

**Share: God created dads (or moms) to help us understand who He is. They are created in God's image—as a picture of God.**

NOTE: If your children have had a negative experience or a troubled relationship with a parent, this point may be difficult to understand. Let kids know that, unlike God, parents aren't perfect. To help children understand this point, explain that dads or moms are created in God's image—but that they don't always do things that make them look like they're created in God's image.

## ACTIVITY 2: God Is Like a Great Dad (or Mom)

**Point: We can learn about God from Mom (or Dad).**

 **Supplies:** You'll need supplies to make a collage (magazines, paper, tape or glue, scissors).

 **Activity:** Form a circle and discuss the following question.
- **What are some of the things that Dad (or Mom) does that teach us about God?** (Dad takes care of us; Mom reads from the Bible; Dad loves us and we learn about God's love.)

**Share: Sometimes we can learn about God by the things Dad (or Mom) does.**

Begin a discussion about how we can see God through Dad or Mom by reading the following comparisons (adjust as necessary for fathers or mothers).
- Dad (or Mom) goes to work and provides for the family—God is our provider
- Dad (or Mom) is strong—God is strong
- Dad (or Mom) protects us—God protects us
- Dad (or Mom) does family nights to teach us—God teaches us
- Dad (or Mom) prays for us—Jesus prays for us
- Dad (or Mom) plays with us—God enjoys being with us
- Mom (or Dad) cooks us food to help us grow—God gives us spiritual food so we will grow
- Mom (or Dad) comforts us when we hurt—God comforts us when we hurt
- Mom gave birth to us—God created us
- Babies are dependent on moms (and dads)—We are dependent on God

After your discussion, gather some magazines, cardboard, tape or glue, and scissors. Work together to find pictures that represent something family members appreciate about Dad (or Mom). Tape or glue the pictures to the cardboard. Then find a place to hang the collage for a week as a celebration of the picture of God that they can see in Dad (or Mom).

Have family members each take a turn hugging Dad (or Mom), and offering a short prayer.

### Age Adjustments

OLDER CHILDREN AND TEENAGERS may prefer expressing themselves through words rather than cutting pictures from magazines. Give older children and teenagers a sheet of paper and ask them to list things they appreciate about Dad (or Mom). Encourage them to list things that help them see a picture of God, such as those discussed during the activity. You may wish to do this yourself, writing a letter to your Dad (or Mom).

## WRAP-UP

Gather everyone in a circle and have family members take turns answering this question: **What's one thing you've learned about God today?**

Next, tell kids you've got a new "Life Slogan" you'd like to share with them.

**Life slogan: Today's Life Slogan is this: "To understand His love, God gave a father's (or mother's) love."** Have family members repeat the slogan two or three times to help them learn it. Then encourage them to practice saying it during the week so they can talk about it at your next family night session.

**Close in Prayer:** Allow time for each family member to share prayer concerns and answers to prayer. Then close your time together with prayer for each concern. Thank God for listening to and caring about us.

Remember to record your prayer requests so you can refer to them in the future as you see God answering them.

### Additional Resource:

*The Children's Discovery Bible* by Charlene Heibert (ages 4-7)

# 7: 4th of July—Freedom and Responsibility

Exploring how God frees us from sin

## Scripture
- Romans 6:18
- Galatians 5:13-15

| ACTIVITY OVERVIEW | | |
|---|---|---|
| Activity | Summary | Pre-Session Prep |
| Activity 1: Wrapped-up Race | Race around the house while becoming increasingly tied-up. | You'll need soft rope or heavy yarn, a watch with a second hand, thread, and a Bible. |
| Activity 2: Freedom | Learn how freedom comes with responsibility as they're tempted to eat candies. | You'll need candies (such as M&Ms), soft rope, and a Bible. |

## Main Points:

- —Jesus took our sins to the cross and freed us from being bound up in sin.
- —When we're set free from sin, we have the freedom to choose, and the responsibility to serve.

**LIFE SLOGAN:** "Jesus sets me free, to live responsibly."

### Make it your own

*In the space provided below, outline the flow and add any additional ideas to guide you through the process of conducting this family night.*

### Prayer & Praise Items

*In the space provided below, list any items you wish to pray about or give praise for during this family night session.*

### Journal

*In the space provided below, capture a record of any fun or meaningful things which happened during this family night session.*

## WARM-UP

**Open with Prayer:** Begin by having a family member pray, asking God to help everyone in the family understand more about Him through this time. After prayer, review your last lesson by asking these questions:

- **What did we learn about in our last lesson?**
- **What was the Life Slogan?**
- **Have your actions changed because of what we learned? If so, how?** Encourage family members to give specific examples of how they've applied learning from the past week.

**Share: Today we're going to talk about how God gives us the freedom to choose, and how we, as God's children, need to be responsible with that freedom.**

## ACTIVITY 1: Wrapped-up Race

**Point: Jesus took our sins to the cross and freed us from being bound up in sin.**

 **Supplies:** You'll need soft rope or heavy yarn, a watch with a second hand, thread, and a Bible.

**Activity:** Using chairs, pillows, toys, and other items, establish a safe race course through your house. You may want to include things to climb over and under, as well as run around.

Walk around the course with your children and show them how to get through it. Then, using a watch with a second hand, time your children as they run the course unencumbered. After announcing how long it took for your children to complete the course, use a soft rope or heavy yarn to tie their feet together and send them on the race a second time. Once again, announce the time. Then tie their hands together and repeat the race. Record the times, then wrap the rope or yarn around each child as if you're turning them into "mummies." It's unlikely that children will be able to complete the course this time, but allow them to attempt it anyway.

Afterward, untie everyone and consider these questions:
- **What happened to your times as you got more and more wrapped up by rope?** (We were slowed down; it took longer to complete the race; we couldn't finish the race.)
- **How is this like the way we get wrapped up in sin and doing things that aren't right?** (When we mess up, we slow down; we can't complete things we're supposed to when we sin.)

Use thread to tie a five- or six-inch diameter loop for each child. Place a loop around each child's wrists and have them attempt to break it. Then repeat the activity with a loop twice as big, wrapping the loop two times before placing it around their wrists. Continue doubling the number of loops in the strand until children can't break free from the thread.

**Share: The more you became bound up by the thread, the more you were controlled by the thread. The same is true with sin. At first, when we sin, we think we can get away with something. But the more we sin, the more we get bound up, and just like this thread, the more we are controlled by sin.**

Have family members list sins that control people. For example: lying, cheating, stealing, gossip; pornography; premarital sex.

**Read** or summarize the following verses: Romans 6:23 (The wages of sin is death, but God's free gift is eternal life in Christ); Romans 5:8 (God demonstrates His love for us in this: While we were still sinners, Christ died for us); and Romans 6:18 (Having been freed from sin, we become slaves to righteousness).

**Share: Jesus took our sins to the cross and freed us from being bound up in sin.**

# ACTIVITY 2: Freedom

**Point:** When we're set free from sin, we have the freedom to choose, and the responsibility to serve.

 **Supplies:** You'll need candies (such as M&Ms), soft rope, and a Bible.

**Activity:** Set a small number of the candies on the floor (no more than 10). Then have your children each sit in a chair, a few feet from the candies. Carefully tie them to their chairs, so they can't reach the candies. Explain that you're tying them up so they won't eat the candies yet.

After a moment of being tied up, untie the children and ask them to choose not to eat the candies while you leave the room. Explain that they will be rewarded if they choose to stay away from the candies.

Leave the room for a minute or two, then return. If some candies are missing, explain that they won't be receiving the reward. If they're all still there, reward family members by getting the rest of the candies out and eating them together.

 Ask:

- **What was the difference between being tied up and not being allowed to eat the candies, and being untied and not being allowed to eat the candies?** (We couldn't even get close to them while tied up; when we were untied, we could have chosen to eat the candies.)

**Share: When I released the ropes, you still had the same instruction: Don't eat the candies. But you were free to choose to obey or disobey. God gives us that same freedom to choose too, but He wants us to be responsible with our choices.**

Have family members list examples from daily life that illustrate the role of freedom and responsibility. For example: freedom to drive a car anywhere, but the responsibility to drive safely; freedom to play outside, but the responsibility to play safely.

 **Read** or summarize Galatians 5:13-15 and ask:

- **How are we to use our freedom?** (To serve God; to serve one another.)

**Share: When we are set free from sin, we have the freedom to choose whom we serve. But as God's children, we also have the responsibility to serve God and do His will.**

## WRAP-UP

Gather everyone in a circle and have family members take turns answering this question: **What's one thing you've learned about God today?**

Next, tell kids you've got a new "Life Slogan" you'd like to share with them.

**Life slogan: Today's Life Slogan is this: "Jesus sets me free, to live responsibly."** Have family members repeat the slogan two or three times to help them learn it. Then encourage them to practice saying it during the week so they can talk about it at your next family night session.

**Close in Prayer:** Allow time for each family member to share prayer concerns and answers to prayer. Then close your time together with prayer for each concern. Thank God for listening to and caring about us.

Remember to record your prayer requests so you can refer to them in the future as you see God answering them.

### Additional Resource:

*In God We Trust: Stories of Faith in American History* by Timothy Crater and Ranelda Hunsicker (ages 7-12)

# ☺ 8: Halloween—Fall Festival

## Exploring how the Gospel brings hope

### Scripture
- Matthew 5:14-16, 23:25-28; Revelation 3:20; 2 Corinthians 5:17; Ephesians 2:10
- Philippians 3:20-21; Luke 24:36-43; Revelation 21:1-4

| ACTIVITY OVERVIEW | | |
|---|---|---|
| Activity | Summary | Pre-Session Prep |
| Activity 1: The Pumpkin Gospel | Carve a pumpkin to learn about the Gospel message. | You'll need a pumpkin, newspapers, a sharp knife, a spoon, a candle, matches, and a Bible. |
| Activity 2: From Pumpkins to Pumpkin Pie | Make a pumpkin pie and learn how God will give us new bodies and a new home. | You'll need ingredients for making pumpkin pie and a Bible. |

## Main Points:

   —We become a new creation when Jesus comes into our heart.

   —Jesus promises us new bodies and a new home in heaven.

**LIFE SLOGAN:** "Jesus in my heart, brings light to every part."

*Make it your own*
In the space provided below, outline the flow and add any additional ideas to guide you through the process of conducting this family night.

*Prayer & Praise Items*
In the space provided below, list any items you wish to pray about or give praise for during this family night session.

*Journal*
In the space provided below, capture a record of any fun or meaningful things which happened during this family night session.

We intentionally have provided more material than we would expect to be used in a single "Family Night" session. You know your family's unique interests and life circumstances best, so feel free to adapt this lesson to meet your family members' needs. Remember, short and simple is better than long and comprehensive.

## WARM-UP

**Open with Prayer:** Begin by having a family member pray, asking God to help everyone in the family understand more about Him through this time. After prayer, review your last lesson by asking these questions:

- **What did we learn about in our last lesson?**
- **What was the Life Slogan?**
- **Have your actions changed because of what we learned? If so, how?** Encourage family members to give specific examples of how they've applied learning from the past week.

**Share:** Every Halloween, people carve pumpkins to make jack-o-lanterns. We're going to carve a pumpkin too, but our pumpkin is going to teach us about the Gospel and God's promise of heaven.

## ACTIVITY 1: The Pumpkin Gospel

**Point:** We become a new creation when Jesus comes into our hearts.

**Supplies:** You'll need a pumpkin, newspapers, a sharp knife, a spoon, a candle, matches, and a Bible.

**Activity:** Prepare a place to do your pumpkin carving. Set newspapers on a table and get out a sharp knife and a large spoon. You'll also need a large bowl.

Cut an opening in the top of the pumpkin and have your kids pull out all of the seeds and scrape out the inside of the pumpkin.

 **Read** Matthew 23:25-28 and Revelation 3:20.

**?** Consider these questions:
- **How is the stuff we pulled out of the pumpkin like sin in our heart?** (They're both yucky; they're inside us; it's sticky and smelly.)
- **How is the way we cleaned out our pumpkin like the way Jesus cleans us out when we confess our sins?** (All the yucky stuff is taken away; Jesus scoops out the sin.)

**📖** Draw a happy face on your pumpkin, then use the sharp knife to carve it out. When your pumpkin has a happy face, **read** aloud 2 Corinthians 5:17 and/or Ephesians 2:10.

**?** Ask:
- **How have we made this pumpkin a "new creation"?** (It has a face now; it used to be just a pumpkin, but now it's a jack-o-lantern.)
- **How do we become a new creation when Jesus comes into our hearts?** (We learn to love Him more; we're no longer filled with yucky stuff; we become God's children.)

**Share: When Jesus comes into our hearts, we become new creations, just as our pumpkin became a new creation. (You may wish to read 2 Corinthians 4:7-10.)**

## Age Adjustments

OLDER CHILDREN AND TEENAGERS will enjoy carving their own pumpkins. You might even want to have a pumpkin carving contest with older children. They may also want to write the message of Matthew 5:14-16 on their pumpkins and place them on the front porch for others to see.

YOUNGER CHILDREN can contribute to the pumpkin carving by helping to draw the faces on the pumpkins before carving. Help younger children use markers to draw the eyes, nose, and mouth for your pumpkin face.

**📖** **Read** aloud Matthew 5:14-16. Then light a candle and place it in the pumpkin. Turn off the room lights and have everyone stand or sit so they can see the light coming through the pumpkin's face.

Discuss how God wants our light to shine before others. (You may also **read** aloud 2 Corinthians 4:6.)

**?** Consider this question:
- **How is the way the candle light comes through the pumpkin like the way God wants our light to shine?** (God wants others to see how much we love Him; God wants our light to be seen by others.)

Sing age-appropriate songs such as "This Little Light of Mine" (younger children) or "Shine Jesus Shine" (older children and teenagers.)

- Place the lighted pumpkin in a closet and ask, **Should we hide our light so others can't see it? Why or why not?**

NOTE: Some of the ideas in this activity were adapted from the children's book, *The Pumpkin Patch Parable,* by Liz Curtis Higgs, published by Tommy Nelson (1995), and her article, *The Pumpkin Patch, in Single-Parent Family* (Focus on the Family, October 1995).

## ACTIVITY 2: From Pumpkins to Pumpkin Pie

**Point: Jesus promises us new bodies and a new home in heaven.**

 **Supplies:** You'll need ingredients for making pumpkin pie and a Bible.

**Activity:** Gather all the necessary ingredients and supplies and work together to make a pumpkin pie. To save time, you might want to purchase a pre-made pie shell from your grocery store. The directions for making pumpkin pie can easily be found on cans of pumpkin pie filling. Do this activity while the pie is baking.

**Share: Those who love God and let their light shine with God's love will get a special gift from God someday. Let's see what the Bible says about that gift.**

**Read** aloud Philippians 3:20-21. Consider these questions:
- **What has Jesus promised those who follow God?** (We will have new bodies; our new bodies will be like His.)
- **What do you think our new bodies will be like?** (They won't have cuts or bruises; they'll be stronger; we won't be ghosts.)

**Read** aloud Luke 24:36-43 and **share: We learn from these verses that Jesus was able to do things that we can't do—such as moving through a wall. Our new bodies will probably be able to do many things we can't do today. We also learn that Jesus ate food and that He wasn't a ghost or spirit, but a person with flesh and bone. Since the Bible tells us**

### Age Adjustments

FOR OLDER CHILDREN AND TEENAGERS, go deeper with your discussion about how our new bodies might be different. Ask them to share thoughts about what they wish would be different about our physical bodies, as well as the world we live in. Dream together about the wondrous possibilities of a new body and a new home to live in with Jesus.

that our new bodies will be like Jesus' we will probably get to enjoy our favorite foods in heaven—and real hugs too!

**Read** aloud Revelation 21:1-4. Then consider these questions:

- **Where will we live when we have new bodies?** (In heaven; with Jesus; on a new earth.)
- **Where is God going to live?** (On the new earth; with us.)
- **What do you think it will be like to have new bodies and live where there is a new heaven and a new earth?** (It will be fun; we'll sing a lot; everyone will be happy.)

Point out that the pumpkins (before carving) represent our lives today. **Share: The change from pumpkin to pumpkin pie represents how God will change us in the future. He will give us new bodies and a new home and we will be with Him forever.**

When the pie is ready, enjoy some pumpkin pie to celebrate God's generous gift of eternal life for those who love Him.

## WRAP-UP

Gather everyone in a circle and have family members take turns answering this question: **What's one thing you've learned about God today?**

Next, tell kids you've got a new "Life Slogan" you'd like to share with them.

**Life slogan: Today's Life Slogan is this: "Jesus in my heart, brings light to every part."** Have family members repeat the slogan two or three time to help them learn it. Then encourage them to practice saying it during the week so they can talk about it at your next family night session.

**Close in Prayer:** Allow time for each family member to share prayer concerns and answers to prayer. Then close your time together with prayer for each concern. Thank God for listening to and caring about us.

Remember to record your prayer requests so you can refer to them in the future as you see God answering them.

### Additional Resources:

*Let's Talk about Heaven* by Debby Anderson (ages 4-7)
*Pocket Book Stories: Heaven* (ages 4-7)

# 9: Halloween—Fighting Hypocrisy

Exploring the importance of acting on what you believe

**Scripture**
- 1 Samuel 16:7
- James 1:22; 2:14-27

| ACTIVITY OVERVIEW | | |
|---|---|---|
| Activity | Summary | Pre-Session Prep |
| Activity 1: Costumes | Wear costumes and learn about when it's not good to pretend. | You'll need costumes. |
| Activity 2: Wearing Masks | God sees who we really are—we can never fool Him. | You'll need construction paper, scissors, crayons or markers, a hat or bowl, and a Bible. |
| Activity 3: Matching Words and Actions | Try saying one thing and doing another, then learning about how our actions are affected by faith. | You'll need a bag of candy, a rope, and a Bible. |

## Main Points:

—God looks beyond the mask and into our heart.

—We prove who we are when what we do reflects what we say.

**LIFE SLOGAN:** "The mask, you see, is hypocrisy."

### Make it your own

In the space provided below, outline the flow and add any additional ideas to guide you through the process of conducting this family night.

### Prayer & Praise Items

In the space provided below, list any items you wish to pray about or give praise for during this family night session.

### Journal

In the space provided below, capture a record of any fun or meaningful things which happened during this family night session.

## Session Tip

We intentionally have provided more material than we would expect to be used in a single "Family Night" session. You know your family's unique interests and life circumstances best, so feel free to adapt this lesson to meet your family members' needs. Remember, short and simple is better than long and comprehensive.

## WARM-UP

**Open with Prayer:** Begin by having a family member pray, asking God to help everyone in the family understand more about Him through this time. After prayer, review your last lesson by asking these questions:

- **What did we learn about in our last lesson?**
- **What was the Life Slogan?**
- **Have your actions changed because of what we learned? If so, how?** Encourage family members to give specific examples of how they've applied learning from the past week.

**Share: This Halloween, we're going to think about masks—but not the kind of masks that we usually think of on Halloween. And we're going to see why it is important to have our actions match our words.**

## ACTIVITY 1: Costumes

**Point: God looks beyond the mask and into our hearts.**

**Supplies:** You'll need costumes.

**Activity:** Have children come to this family night dressed in typical Halloween costumes. Children may dress up using clothes they already have if you don't have any regular costumes. Help them as necessary so they can wear something fun, and be sure the costumes include a mask if at all possible. You'll want to be sure and dress up to join in on the fun.

When everyone is ready, take turns guessing who each person came dressed up as. Then (if appropriate), have each family member take a minute to act in the way the person they're dressed up to be would act. For example, someone dressed up as a cowboy might

pretend to ride on a horse. Someone dressed up as a ballerina might dance.

 Then consider these questions:
- **What was fun about dressing up in a costume?** (I like to pretend to be someone else; I like how I look; it's fun to look different.)
- **Why do people pretend to be someone they're not?** (They want to see what it's like; they think it's fun.)

**Share: When we dress up for Halloween, we do so because it's fun. When we put on a mask, it's to hide who we are and surprise friends and neighbors. But when people put on different kinds of masks and pretend to be someone they're not, that's not a good thing. Let's learn more about the bad kinds of masks.**

## ACTIVITY 2: Wearing Masks

**Point: God sees who we really are—we can never fool Him.**

**Supplies:** You'll need construction paper, scissors, crayons or makers, a hat or bowl, and a Bible.

### Age Adjustments

OLDER CHILDREN AND TEENAGERS are experts at understanding (and often practicing) hypocrisy. Use this activity time to springboard into a discussion of the pressure to fit in and how that contributes to the temptation to "put on a mask" at school, home, work, and even church. Help your children see the value of being true to oneself even when the pressure to put on a mask is great.

**Activity:** Give each member of the family a stack of construction paper, scissors, and crayons or markers. Place a number of pieces of paper in a hat or bowl with a different name on each. The names can be people (Dad, Mom, Grandpa, etc.), animals (bird, dog, cat, etc.), or famous characters (Mickey Mouse, Mr. Magoo, etc.). Take turns drawing names and creating a mask to look like the name on the paper. (You may need to assist younger children.) Then take turns wearing the masks and trying to guess who/what the mask is supposed to represent.

 Then discuss the following questions:
- **Who was the champion mask maker? Why?**
- **When we were wearing our masks, was it easier or harder to show our true selves? Why?**

**Share: In ancient days, actors on a stage wore masks and were called hypocrites. Hypocrites were those who pretended to be some-**

one they were not. **In what ways do we sometimes pretend to be someone we are not?** (When we pretend to be nice or mean. When we lie. When we act like we don't care, but we really do, etc.)

 **Read** aloud 1 Samuel 16:7. Then ask:
- **Does the Lord look at our outward actions/appearance or at our hearts?** (Our hearts.)

## ACTIVITY 3: Matching Words and Actions

**Point: We prove who we are when what we do reflects what we say.**

 **Supplies:** You'll need a bag of candy, a rope, and a Bible.

**Activity:** Have family members take turns attempting the following actions:
- Shake your head no while saying "yes."
- Nod yes while saying "no way."
- Say "I'm not going to jump up and down" while jumping up and down.
- Say "I would never stomp my feet" while stomping their feet.

You may wish to add some of your own ideas, or have family members come up with a few similar ideas where the words and actions don't match.

 After trying some of these actions, ask:
- **What was it like to do one thing and say another?** (It was fun; it was difficult; I didn't like it.)
- **How is this like the way some people behave in real life?** (They say they love God but they don't act that way; they say they are Christians but don't live like it.)

**Share: People who say one thing and do another are called hypocrites. God wants us to be true to what we say and who we are. If we say that we are Christians and that we love God, our actions will reflect that.**

Tie the rope to the bag of candy and place both on the floor at one end of the room. Ask children to push the candy to the other end of the room while leaving the rope straight and touching only the loose end of the rope (it can't be done). After a moment of frustration, ask children to take turns pulling the candy bag to the other end of the room, again, touching only the loose end of the rope and keeping the rope straight. This should be quite simple.

Then form a circle as you enjoy the candy together. Ask:
• **Why was it impossible to move the candy the first time?**
(Because the rope is no good for pushing things; because we couldn't keep the rope straight.)

**Read** aloud James 1:22 and 2:14-27. **Then share: When we become Christians we tell God that we want to follow His will. And when we follow God, our actions (or works) match what we say. In other words, when we say we love God, we choose to do things that God would want us to do.**

Have children think of things that God might want them to do, and things God might not want them to do.

**Share: Sometimes, people try to reach God by doing all the right things—they think that if they do great works, God will let them into His family. But this is kind of like trying to push the candy using the rope: our works or actions can't make us Christians. But when we say with our words that we accept Christ as our Savior, we are called to "pull the candy bag" or do the things God wants us to do. We become members of God's family and begin to make our actions match those that are appropriate for God's family.**

## WRAP-UP

Gather everyone in a circle and have family members take turns answering this question: **What's one thing you've learned about God today?**

Next, tell kids you've got a new "Life Slogan" you'd like to share with them.

**Life slogan: Today's Life Slogan is this: "The mask, you see, is hypocrisy."** Have family members repeat the slogan two or three times to help them learn it. Then encourage them to practice saying it during the week so they can talk about it at your next family night session.

**Close in Prayer:** Allow time for each family member to share prayer concerns and answers to prayer. Then close your time together with prayer for each concern. Thank God for listening to and caring about us.

Remember to record your prayer requests so you can refer to them in the future as you see God answering them.

**Additional Resources:**

*Christian's Journey* (ages 4-8)
Full Armor of God playset (ages 3-11)

# @ 10: Thanksgiving—Giving Thanks

## Exploring how to develop the spirit of thanksgiving

### Scripture
- 1 Timothy 6:9-10; Philippians 4:4-7, 11-13
- 1 Timothy 6:6-8

| ACTIVITY OVERVIEW | | |
|---|---|---|
| Activity | Summary | Pre-Session Prep |
| Activity 1: Water Glass Parable | Draw pictures and learn what it means to be content. | You'll need a glass, water, paper, crayons, and a Bible. |
| Activity 2: Thanksgiving Treasure Hunt | Go on a treasure hunt to find things they're thankful for. | You'll need 3x5 cards, pencils, fun prizes, and a Bible. |

## Main Points:
—When we focus on what we don't have, we feel unhappy.

—The treasure of a thankful heart is contentment.

**LIFE SLOGAN:** "To give thanks and be content, doesn't cost a cent!"

### Make it your own
*In the space provided below, outline the flow and add any additional ideas to guide you through the process of conducting this family night.*

### Prayer & Praise Items
*In the space provided below, list any items you wish to pray about or give praise for during this family night session.*

### Journal
*In the space provided below, capture a record of any fun or meaningful things which happened during this family night session.*

## Session Tip

We intentionally have provided more material than we would expect to be used in a single "Family Night" session. You know your family's unique interests and life circumstances best, so feel free to adapt this lesson to meet your family members' needs. Remember, short and simple is better than long and comprehensive.

### WARM-UP

**Open with Prayer:** Begin by having a family member pray, asking God to help everyone in the family understand more about Him through this time. After prayer, review your last lesson by asking these questions:

- **What did we learn about in our last lesson?**
- **What was the Life Slogan?**
- **Have your actions changed because of what we learned? If so, how?** Encourage family members to give specific examples of how they've applied learning from the past week.

**Share:** Today we're going to talk about things that we're thankful for. We're also going to learn what it means to be content.

## ACTIVITY 1: Water Glass Parable

**Point: When we focus on what we don't have, we get unhappy.**

 **Supplies:** You'll need a glass, water, paper, crayons, and a Bible.

**Activity:** Fill a glass half full of water and set it on the table. Then ask family members whether the glass is half full or half empty. After everyone responds, point out that whether the glass is half full or half empty depends on how you look at it.

Give each family member a sheet of paper and a crayon or other drawing instrument. Have each person draw a large half-filled glass on their paper. Then have everyone list or draw

### Age Adjustments

OLDER CHILDREN AND TEENAGERS will relate well to this discussion on contentment. With all of the pressures they probably feel from peers about the kinds of clothes to wear, among other things, they're experts on wanting "more." Use this time to help your children differentiate between those things that are "needs" and those that are "wants." Ask older children and teenagers how they think their lives would be different if they had the "want" items. Then explore together ways to begin focusing on being thankful for what they have rather than wishing for what they don't. One idea is to have your children choose one item they already own and spend a day in thanks for that item. Kids may even discover they have more than they need and may come up with a plan to share some of their "stuff" with others.

pictures of things that they already own on top of the water-filled portion of the drawing. Have them list or draw pictures of things they want on the empty portion of the drawing.

Then discuss:

- **How does it feel when you look at the things that you already have?** (I feel lucky; it makes me feel happy.)
- **How does it feel when you look at the things that you want?** (It makes me feel sad; it makes me feel like I want those items.)
- **What happens when we focus on the things we don't have?** (We feel sad; it makes us unhappy.)

 **Read** aloud 1 Timothy 6:9-10. **Then share: The love of money or things we buy with money can get us into lots of trouble. We think we're going to be happy when we get the things we want, but when we focus on those things, we just get unhappy.**

 Ask:

- **What happens when we think about the things we already have and are thankful?** (We're happy; we feel good; we remember how blessed we are.)

 **Read** aloud 1 Thessalonians 5:18 and discuss how we ought to obey God's will for us. Then **read** aloud Philippians 4:11-13 and discuss how contentment is the result of being thankful.

## ACTIVITY 2: Thanksgiving Treasure Hunt

**Point: The treasure of a thankful heart is contentment.**

**Supplies:** You'll need 3x5 cards, pencils, fun prizes, and a Bible.

**Activity:** Ask family members this question:

- **What does it mean to be discontent?** (It means you're not happy; it means you always want more.)

**Share: Being discontent means always feeling like you don't have enough stuff. For example, let's imagine that you have a toy you really like. While watching television, you see an advertisement for an even "better" toy. Do you feel like you have to have that toy? That feeling is what it's like to be discontent. Even though you have a perfectly good toy, you always want one more.**

Have family members share the last time they were discontent and why. Then explain that you're going to find a medicine to help fight discontentment.

Tell your children that you're going to go on a thanksgiving treasure hunt. Explain that you'll go several places around your home (or town—this activity is a great excuse for a visit to your church, your children's school, and your favorite restaurant or entertainment hot spot). At each place, family members will need to think of things they're thankful for. Let everyone know you'll give a prize to the people who think of the most thankful things. Take a pack of 3x5 cards with you as you go around your home or community and have older kids list things they're thankful for at each location. Younger children can draw pictures of things they're thankful for, or may need help from you in listing those things. Plan on giving a prize to everyone for thinking of thankful things. Prize ideas will vary, but choose items that your family members will enjoy and say "thanks" for.

Here are a few "around town" locations you might visit and some things family members might be thankful for at each:

School—education, friends, teachers
Hospital—doctors, babies, medicine, health
Post office—letters, presents, grandparents
Church—Jesus, friends, the Bible, learning about God
Your home—family members, food, toys

When you get home, or finish visiting different rooms in your house, **read** Ephesians 5:20. Reiterate Paul's message to "always give thanks for everything." Then review 1 Timothy 6:6-8. **Share: Being greedy means wanting more when we're already full. Paul says he's learned to be content or happy with what he has. Let's talk about the things we listed or drew on our cards and how thankful we are for those things.**

Spend time reading or looking at the items on the 3x5 cards and discuss how the treasure of a thankful heart is contentment.

Take a box (a shoe box will do) and have family members help decorate it to look like a treasure box. Place all the cards in that box.

## Age Adjustments

FOR YOUNGER CHILDREN, consider a simple exercise to help them understand the value of being thankful and content. Offer a single candy (such as an M&M) to your younger child. If he or she says "thanks" and eats it without asking for more, explain how that's like being content, or happy, with what they have or are given. If your child asks for more, explain that you're only offering one candy. If your child persists, explain how wanting more than you have means being discontent or unhappy with what you have. Help your younger child see that we can be thankful for all the things we're given and be happy with what we have.

Encourage family members to pull out a card and read it whenever they're feeling discontent.

### WRAP-UP

Gather everyone in a circle and have family members take turns answering this question: **What's one thing you've learned about God today?**

Next, tell kids you've got a new "Life Slogan" you'd like to share with them.

**Life slogan: Today's Life Slogan is this: "To give thanks and be content, doesn't cost a cent!"** Have family members repeat the slogan two or three times to help them learn it. Then encourage them to practice saying it during the week so they can talk about it at your next family night session.

**Close in Prayer:** Allow time for each family member to share prayer concerns and answers to prayer. Then close your time together with prayer for each concern. Thank God for listening to and caring about us.

Remember to record your prayer requests so you can refer to them in the future as you see God answering them.

### Additional Resources:

*Helpful Hal's Treasury of Christian Value*s by Michael Waite (ages 4-7)
My Giving Bank (ages 3 and up)

# 11: Thanksgiving—An Attitude of Gratitude

Exploring how to give thanks and not take blessings for granted

## Scripture
- 1 Thessalonians 5:18
- 1 Chronicles 16:4-36

| ACTIVITY OVERVIEW | | |
|---|---|---|
| Activity | Summary | Pre-Session Prep |
| Activity 1: Eye Thank You | Try to eat a meal without using your hands or eyes. | You'll need a typical family meal, cloth strips, and a Bible. |
| Activity 2: Things I'm Thankful For | Pass around popcorn and think of things they're thankful for. | You'll need unpopped popcorn, a bowl, supplies for popping popcorn, and a Bible. |

## Main Points:

    —We must give thanks in all circumstances.

    —We have much to be thankful for.

**LIFE SLOGAN:** "We can have an attitude of gratitude."

### Make it your own
*In the space provided below, outline the flow and add any additional ideas to guide you through the process of conducting this family night.*

### Prayer & Praise Items
*In the space provided below, list any items you wish to pray about or give praise for during this family night session.*

### Journal
*In the space provided below, capture a record of any fun or meaningful things which happened during this family night session.*

## Session Tip

We intentionally have provided more material than we would expect to be used in a single "Family Night" session. You know your family's unique interests and life circumstances best, so feel free to adapt this lesson to meet your family members' needs. Remember, short and simple is better than long and comprehensive.

### WARM-UP

**Open with Prayer:** Begin by having a family member pray, asking God to help everyone in the family understand more about Him through this time. After prayer, review your last lesson by asking these questions:

- **What did we learn about in our last lesson?**
- **What was the Life Slogan?**
- **Have your actions changed because of what we learned? If so, how?** Encourage family members to give specific examples of how they've applied learning from the past week.

**Share: Today we're going to find out how many wonderful things we can be thankful for and how we can be thankful in all circumstances.**

## ACTIVITY 1: Eye Thank You

**Point: We must give thanks in all circumstances.**

**Supplies:** You'll need a typical family meal, cloth strips, and a Bible.

**Activity:** Open your family night with a quick recap of the story of the first Thanksgiving. You can use the following as a guide for telling your family the story.

### The Story of Thanksgiving

Many years ago, when only the Indians lived in America, people from a faraway land came to America to live. They came because they wanted to have the freedom to follow God, and they weren't allowed to do that where they had been living. These Colonists (we also call them

## Age Adjustments

Ask OLDER CHILDREN AND TEENAGERS to share times when they felt least thankful at school, home, work, and at church. These could be times when they got a bad grade on a test; were yelled at by a teacher; got "burned" by a friend; and so on. Then have older children and teenagers take a fresh look at each of those situations to find at least three things they could be thankful for. Encourage your children to change their perspective from one of always seeing the negative aspects of a situation to being thankful for all that is good—even in the worst of situations.

Pilgrims) settled on the East Coast at a place called Plymouth Rock. In order to provide food for their families, the Colonists planned to farm the land and grow lots of vegetables, grains to make bread, and fruits. However, the first winter was very difficult and nearly half of the Colonists died.

At the end of the following harvest season, the governor set aside a day of fasting and prayer to show thanks go God for providing food for them. Then they planned a huge feast to celebrate their good growing season.

People spent many days preparing for this feast. Indians and Colonists alike shared in this great time of thanks. And this tradition continues today in the holiday we call Thanksgiving.

 Consider these questions:

- **Do you think it was easy for the Colonists to be thankful after losing half of their people in that terrible first winter? Why or why not?** (No, because they didn't have much to be thankful for; yes, because they still could be thankful for those people who survived.)
- **When has it been difficult for you to be thankful?** (When I get in trouble; when someone I care about is sick; when I'm having a bad day.)

 **Read** aloud 1 Thessalonians 5:18. Paraphrase if necessary for younger children.

 Ask:

- **What does God tell us to do in this passage?** (Give thanks in all circumstances; always be thankful.)
- **Is it easy to always be thankful? Why or why not?** (No, when things go wrong I don't feel thankful; yes, I know I can be thankful even when things are bad.)

Sit at your dinner table to enjoy a meal together. One at a time, blindfold each family member and tie his or her hands to the chair. Have fun watching everyone try to eat the meal while "handicapped" in this way. (It may be fun to prepare food particularly difficult to eat without your hands or eyes.)

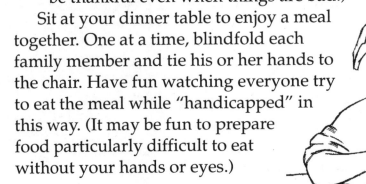

**?** While you are eating dinner, discuss these questions:

- **Do we remember to be thankful for our eyes and hands very often?** (No, it is easy to forget to be thankful for these things.)
- **What other things do we often take for granted and forget to be thankful for?** (Our legs, feet, hearing, smell, taste, etc.)

**Share: Thanksgiving is designed to remind us to be thankful for the blessings God gives, even those things we often take for granted— such as our health, food, house, clothes, and our ability to see, walk, talk, hear, etc.**

## ACTIVITY 2: Things I'm Thankful For

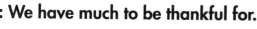: **We have much to be thankful for.**

 **Supplies:** You'll need unpopped popcorn, a bowl, supplies for popping popcorn, and a Bible.

**Activity:** Sit in a circle on the floor. Give each family member three to five pieces of unpopped popcorn. Place a bowl with the remaining unpopped popcorn in the center of the circle.

Tell family members they must think of things to be thankful for, share those things, and drop one piece of unpopped popcorn into the bowl for each idea. (If you have an especially thankful family, you may wish to give each person more pieces of unpopped popcorn).

When people have exhausted their thankful ideas, take the unpopped popcorn and . . . pop it. Bring over the hot popcorn and **share: Just as taking unpopped popcorn and heating it up makes a tasty new treat we can enjoy, taking good and bad situations alike and finding things to be thankful makes our lives enjoyable and "tasty."**

Have family members each share one or more reasons they're thankful for the person on their left. Take a moment for prayer and allow all family members to thank God for any of the things they've talked about during this family night activity. Then dive into the cooked popcorn together.

**Read** aloud or summarize 1 Chronicles 16:4-36. Then consider these questions:

- **Why does David give thanks to God in this passage?**

(Because of God's strength; because He has done miracles; because He is holy.)

• **What have we learned about thankfulness?** (We can be thankful in all situations; we have a lot to be thankful for.)

## Age Adjustments

Help YOUNGER CHILDREN see the many things we can be thankful for by playing a simple game. Just have children say "Thank you God for _____" and fill in the blank with any item that you point to. For example, if you point to a picture of a sunset on the wall, children might respond, "Thank you God for sunsets (or pictures)." Repeat this using lots of objects in the room, then end the game by pointing to each family member.

**Share: In 1 Chronicles, David shares many reasons he is thankful to God. We've also learned that there are many reasons to be thankful. During this Thanksgiving season, and in the weeks and months that follow, let's do our best to be people who are thankful, rather than people who are complainers.**

## WRAP-UP

Gather everyone in a circle and have family members take turns answering this question: **What's one thing you've learned about God today?**

Next, tell kids you've got a new "Life Slogan" you'd like to share with them.

**Life slogan: Today's Life Slogan is this: "We can have an attitude of gratitude."** Have family members repeat the slogan two or three times to help them learn it. Then encourage them to practice saying it during the week so they can talk about it at your next family night session.

**Close in Prayer:** Allow time for each family member to share prayer concerns and answers to prayer. Then close your time together with prayer for each concern. Thank God for listening to and caring about us.

Remember to record your prayer requests so you can refer to them in the future as you see God answering them.

### Additional Resources:

*Baby Bible Devotions* by Cathy Davis (ages 1-3)
*Toddlers Devotions* by V. Gilbert Beers (ages 1-4)
*Devotions for the Sandbox Set* by Jane Morton (ages 2-5)
*Kids-Life Devotions* (ages 4-7)
*Caution: Dangerous Devotions* by Jackie Perseghetti (ages 8 and up)

# ⊚ 12: Christmas—God Became a Man

## Exploring the real meaning of Christmas

### Scripture
- Luke 1:26-38
- John 14:9-10

| ACTIVITY OVERVIEW | | |
|---|---|---|
| **Activity** | **Summary** | **Pre-Session Prep** |
| Activity 1: God's Choice | Choose a Christmas tree and learn how God chose Mary. | You'll want to plan this activity for the day you get a Christmas tree (or other Christmas decoration). You'll also need a Bible and hot chocolate. |
| Activity 2: Pet Tricks | Teach a pet a new trick and learn why God became human. | You'll need the cooperation of a house pet (dog, cat, etc.) or a goldfish from a local pet store, and a Bible. |

## Main Points:

— When God sent Jesus to earth, God chose me.

— God became a man so we could understand His love.

**LIFE SLOGAN:** "God became a man, so His love we'd understand."

*Make it your own*
In the space provided below, outline the flow and add any additional ideas to guide you through the process of conducting this family night.

*Prayer & Praise Items*
In the space provided below, list any items you wish to pray about or give praise for during this family night session.

*Journal*
In the space provided below, capture a record of any fun or meaningful things which happened during this family night session.

## Session Tip

We intentionally have provided more material than we would expect to be used in a single "Family Night" session. You know your family's unique interests and life circumstances best, so feel free to adapt this lesson to meet your family members' needs. Remember, short and simple is better than long and comprehensive.

## WARM-UP

**Open with Prayer:** Begin by having a family member pray, asking God to help everyone in the family understand more about Him through this time. After prayer, review your last lesson by asking these questions:

- **What did we learn about in our last lesson?**
- **What was the Life Slogan?**
- **Have your actions changed because of what we learned? If so, how?** Encourage family members to give specific examples of how they've applied learning from the past week.

**Share: Today we're going to talk about the true meaning of Christmas.**

## ACTIVITY 1: God's Choice

**Point: When God sent Jesus to earth, God chose me.**

**Supplies:** This activity is tied directly to a common family tradition of choosing a Christmas tree together. If you can do this activity on the same night that you choose your tree, great! If you already have a tree, you can do a similar activity using a wreath or other decoration. Plan to go as a family to choose this item so your children will have an opportunity to experience "choosing something special." You'll also need a Bible and hot chocolate.

**Activity:** Prepare for a family outing to choose a special Christmas tree (or other Christmas decoration). Before you head out, talk with your family about the importance of choosing a tree you all think is special. Make a list of the criteria you will use to choose a tree (how tall, what type, cost, etc.). Then head out to Christmas tree lots (or to a place where you can cut your own tree) and get your special tree.

When you return home, enjoy some hot chocolate and set up your tree. After the tree-decorating time, ask family members to share what was involved in getting a special tree for your family. For example: We looked and looked; we considered different trees; we got excited about one or more trees; we brought a tree home; we made a choice.

 **Read** aloud Luke 1:26-38. Then consider these questions:

• **What choice did God have to make in this passage?** (Who would be the mother of His son, Jesus.)

 **Read** aloud (or have a family member recite from memory) John 3:16. Then discuss:

• **Why did God send Jesus as a baby into our world at Christmas?** (So He could get to know us; so we would have eternal life.)

## Age Adjustments

YOUNGER CHILDREN will enjoy this activity more if they're truly involved in the decision-making process for choosing your Christmas tree. Since younger children may not understand things like "cost" or "appropriate size" when it comes to choosing a tree, they may begin saying "let's get that one" to the biggest, most expensive, or driest tree on the lot. You can assure their success in helping you choose a tree by pre-selecting a few trees that fit your basic criteria and allowing them to choose from among those trees. Knowing that they really helped to choose a tree can prepare younger children for the main point in this activity—as well as give them a self-esteem boost.

**Share:** When God sent Jesus to the earth as a baby, He chose us. Let's look at how the words in John 3:16 match up with our experience choosing a Christmas tree:

"God so loved the world . . . " Just as we were excited about our Christmas tree, God is excited about us and loves us.

". . . that He gave His only Son, that whoever believes in Him should not perish . . . " Just as we chose a Christmas tree, God chose us.

 ". . . but have eternal life." Just as we brought our tree home, decorated it and will celebrate Christmas with it, God wants to bring us to be home with Him, decorate us in new bodies, and celebrate with us forever. (Optional: **Read** Matthew 14:2-3 to reinforce this point.)

# ACTIVITY 2: Pet Tricks

**Point: God became a man so we could understand His love.**

 **Supplies:** You'll need to buy an inexpensive goldfish if you don't have one already or get your dog or cat to "play along," and a Bible.

**Activity:** At the beginning of your family night, ask the children to train your house pet or the goldfish you've purchased to do a new trick. If the kids are struggling for ideas, suggest that they try to get the fish to jump out of the water or the dog or cat to jump through a Hula Hoop or roll a rubber ball across the room with its nose. Bring necessary props along.

Give the kids just about five minutes and watch them as they try to talk the fish/animal into "performing." Most likely, unless the animal is exceptionally intelligent, the kids will soon be frustrated at their lack of success. Discuss the following questions:

- **How did the fish/animal respond?** (Confused; they didn't understand.)
- **How could you get the fish/animal to understand?** (If children don't know how to respond, ask if any of the following ideas would work: talk to them; write them a letter; call them on the phone.)

**Share: The only way we could truly communicate with our animals would be if we could become animals ourselves.**

God is bigger than us, just as we're bigger and smarter than our pets (most of the time!). We might be afraid if God tried to talk to us with His big voice. And we might not understand what He would say to us. So what do you think God would do if He wanted to tell us that He loved us and that we didn't need to be afraid? He would become a man!

 **Read** aloud John 14:9-10. Then summarize by **saying: God became a man—Jesus—so we could get to know and understand God's love for us.**

## WRAP-UP

Gather everyone in a circle and have family members take turns answering this question: **What's one thing you've learned about God today?**

Next, tell kids you've got a new "Life Slogan" you'd like to share with them.

**Life slogan: Today's Life Slogan is this: "God became a man, so His love we'd understand."** Have family members repeat the slogan two or three times to help them learn it. Then encourage them to practice saying it during the week so they can talk about it at your next family night session.

**Close in Prayer:** Allow time for each family member to share prayer concerns and answers to prayer. Then close your time together with prayer for each concern. Thank God for listening to and caring about us.

Remember to record your prayer requests so you can refer to them in the future as you see God answering them.

## Additional Resources:

*Before the Stars Were Made* by Lois Rock (ages 4-7)

*My Son, My Savior* by Calvin Miller (family reading)

*My Jesus Pocketbook: Christmas Is Coming, Joy to the World, Very Special Birthday* (ages 4-7)

*The Toddlers Bible Christmas Book* by V. Gilbert Beers (ages 1-3)

*The Gift of the Magi* by O. Henry, retold by Penelope Stokes (family reading)

*Sleepy Jesus* by Pennie Kidd (ages 3-5)

*The 25 Days of Christmas* by Rebecca Hayford Bauer (family Advent book)

*A Night the Stars Danced for Joy* by Bob Hartman (ages 4-7)

*The Children's Discovery Bible* by Charlene Heibert (ages 4-7)

*The Picture Bible* by Iva Hoth (ages 8-12)

Bible Greats: Nativity playset (ages 4-10)

# 13: Christmas—An Advent Celebration

## Explore the meaning and purpose of the season of Advent

*NOTE: This family night lesson includes four activities to spread out during the four weeks of Advent leading up to Christmas. You may choose to use them in conjunction with an advent candle lighting ceremony.*

**Scripture**
• John 3:16; Matthew 1:21-23; Romans 5:8; Mark 16:12-14; John 1:14, 18

### ACTIVITY OVERVIEW

| Activity | Summary | Pre-Session Prep |
|---|---|---|
| Week 1: How Much God Loves Us | Create a wreath and learn about God's love for them. | You'll need a Bible. (Optional: You may also need supplies to make an Advent wreath, including greenery and four candles.) |
| Week 2: Born to Die | Create a cross and discover the reason God came to earth. | You'll need a large piece of cardboard, markers, scissors, tape, and a Bible. |
| Week 3: Eternal Life | Learn how long they've been alive and imagine how long eternity is. | You'll need a calculator, a calendar, a sheet of paper, and a pencil. |
| Week 4: If Only . . . | Listen to a parable and discover why God came as a man. | You'll need winter clothing, bread crumbs, and a Bible. |

**Main Points:**

—Jesus came to show us how much God loves us.

—Jesus came to die for our sins.

—Jesus came to give us eternal life.

—Jesus came to teach us about God.

**LIFE SLOGAN:** "Emmanuel, God is with us!"

### Make it your own
In the space provided below, outline the flow and add any additional ideas to guide you through the process of conducting this family night.

### Prayer & Praise Items
In the space provided below, list any items you wish to pray about or give praise for during this family night session.

### Journal
In the space provided below, capture a record of any fun or meaningful things which happened during this family night session.

We intentionally have provided more material than we would expect to be used in a single "Family Night" session. You know your family's unique interests and life circumstances best, so feel free to adapt this lesson to meet your family members' needs. Remember, short and simple is better than long and comprehensive.

## WARM-UP

**Open with Prayer:** Begin by having a family member pray, asking God to help everyone in the family understand more about Him through this time. After prayer, review your last lesson by asking these questions:

- **What did we learn about in our last lesson?**
- **What was the Life Slogan?**
- **Have your actions changed because of what we learned? If so, how?** Encourage family members to give specific examples of how they've applied learning from the past week.

**Share: Today we're going to learn about the Advent season and why God sent the Baby Jesus to earth.**

# WEEK 1: How Much God Loves Us

**Point: Jesus came to show us how much God loves us.**

**Supplies:** You'll need a Bible. (Optional: You may also need supplies to make an Advent wreath, including greenery and four candles.)

**Activity:** Open this activity by asking children if they know what "advent" means. **Then share: "Advent" is a word that means "coming soon." We call the Christmas season the "Advent" season for two reasons. First, it's the "coming soon" of Christmas, or Jesus' birthday. And second, it's a time to remember that Jesus promised He would return someday. We're going to spend the next four weeks of the Advent season exploring why God chose to send Jesus to earth, and what that means for us.**

Place a box in the middle of the room and ask your family members to go and collect something that is very important to them to put in the box. You may wish to help younger children find a toy or stuffed animal that they value. When everyone has placed an item in the box, take the box and place it by the front door. **Say: We value these things very much. But how much more important would they be to people who are less fortunate or who have fewer things?**

You may hear complaints as kids begin to wonder what you're doing with their stuff. Allow the complaining, but don't tell anyone what your plans are until after you discuss this question:

• **How would it feel if we gave these things to people who don't have much?** (I'd be sad to see my things go; I would be happy for them; I don't want to give my toy away.)

**Share: When we give something away that we value or truly love, that's called a sacrifice. God showed His love for us in a deep way when He sent His Son, Jesus, to be born, live, and then die for our sins. That was an incredible sacrifice and a beautiful picture of God's great love.**

**Read** John 3:16. Tell children that they don't have to give up their valuable items, but that you'd like to keep them in the box for a couple days as a reminder of the incredible love that God has for us.

If you have the supplies, work together to create an Advent wreath, complete with four candles (and an optional fifth candle for the middle of the wreath). During this family night, or on the first Sunday in Advent, light the first candle. Then, each following week, light one additional candle until all four are lit on the fourth Sunday of Advent. Some families also have a fifth candle, or the "Christ" candle which they only light on Christmas Day (along with all the other candles).

When lighting the candles each week, reinforce the true meaning of the coming of Jesus by saying together, "Emmanuel, God is with us!" **Read** Matthew 1:21-23 together and point out that Jesus was called Emmanuel because He was God with us. Also, if you know the Christmas hymn, "O Come, O Come, Emmanuel," it may be good to sing it at this point.

# WEEK 2: Born to Die

**Point: Jesus came to die for our sins.**

 **Supplies:** You'll need a large piece of cardboard, markers, scissors, tape, and a Bible.

**Activity:** Have family members help you create a large cardboard cross. Then take turns drawing symbols or words on the cross to indicate sins or wrongdoings from the past week. Let family members know that they don't need to write out the specific sin, but that God will understand the symbols or pictures that they draw. You'll want to help younger children think about things they might have done that would "make God sad."

 When everyone has written or drawn something on the cross, read Romans 5:8. **Then share: God sent His son, Jesus, to die on the cross. But when Jesus died on the cross, He took away all of our sins.**

Use a big red marker to write the word "Jesus" across all the images and words on your cardboard cross.

 Ask:

• **What does it feel like to know that Jesus died to take away our sins?** (It makes me feel good; I'm sad that He had to die.)

**Share: Because Jesus died on the cross, we can be forgiven for all that we do that's wrong. But God doesn't just forgive us, He forgets our sins too.**

Have a volunteer pray, thanking God for sending Jesus to die for our sins.

# WEEK 3: Eternal Life

**Point: Jesus came to give us eternal life.**

 **Supplies:** You'll need a calculator, a calendar, a sheet of paper, and a pencil.

**Activity:** Using a calculator and a calendar, help your children discover approximately how many months, weeks, days, hours, and even minutes they've been alive. Unsure of how to do this? Figure out how many months a child has been alive, then multiply by 4 to determine the approximate number of weeks. Then multiply that number by 7 to determine the number of days. Multiply that number by 24 to determine hours. Multiply the hours by 60 to determine minutes. And multiply the number of minutes by 60 to find out seconds.

Write these numbers on a sheet of paper next to the family member's name and ask children to comment on how big the numbers are. Then ask children to tell you things they know about "time." Consider these questions:

- **What is the longest time you can think of?** (100 years; a million years.)
- **What are some things you wish you could spend lots of time doing?** (Playing with my toys; swimming; playing games with my family; playing baseball.)

 Ask children to tell you how long "forever" is. **Read** aloud Mark 16:12-14. **Share: God loves us so much that He wants to spend a long time with us. Because He sent Jesus to be born, die, and rise again from the dead, we can have eternal life—or "forever" with Jesus. If we love Jesus, we'll go to be with Him forever when we die— or when He comes to earth again as He promised in the Bible.**

End this activity by dreaming big dreams about the wonders of living eternally with Jesus.

## WEEK 4: If Only...

**Point: Jesus came to teach us about God.**

**Supplies:** You'll need winter clothing, bread crumbs, and a Bible.

**Activity:** For this activity, you'll want to select one or more children to play the parts of birds in the story that follows. You or another parent will need to play the part of the man in the story. Use the winter clothing and bread crumbs as you act out the story for your children. You may read the story and act it out as is, or paraphrase it for your family.

Begin by helping children imagine it is a blizzardy day. Determine where the man's house is and where the window is that he can look out of to see the cold, blowing snow. Have children make sounds of blowing wind as you begin the story. Encourage them to act out the actions as you tell the story.

**Begin:** It was Christmas Eve. A man and his wife stood by the door watching the cold, blowing snow. "Come with me to church," the wife pleaded. "No. I simply can't understand what Christmas is all about. What does it mean, anyway, that God became a man? No, you go. I'll stay here, warming myself by the fireplace."

As the door closed behind his wife, the man sat down near the fireplace to watch the drifting snow. Suddenly, he heard a thud near the front window. He got up, walked over to the window, and looked down. There, on the ground, were some birds. "They must have been trying to fly through the window," the man thought. Being a kind person, he tried to think of something he could do to keep the birds from freezing.

"The barn! That would be a nice shelter." He put on his heavy winter coat and boots and fought his way through the snow to the barn. He turned on the barn lights and opened the door, but the birds didn't come in. He went back to the house and got some bread. Carefully, he laid out bread crumbs leading from the shivering birds to the barn. Still they ignored him. He tried waving his arms and yelling to them, "Come here, it's warm here!" But the birds didn't move. In fact, they seemed frightened of him.

Puzzled and sad, the man thought, "If only I could be a bird myself for a moment, perhaps I could lead them to the barn."

Just then the church bells rang, singing out the joy of Christmas. The man stood quietly, then dropped to his knees in the snow. "Now I understand," he whispered. He looked up into the sky and continued, "Now I see why You had to become a man."

Ask family members to tell what they thought of the story. Consider these questions:

- **Why did the man finally understand why God became a man?** (Because he wanted to become a bird to save the birds; because he knew that was the only way to reach men and women.)

- **How might people have reacted if God had come down to us in a different form, not as a baby who would grow up to a man?** (People might have been scared; they wouldn't trust Him; they wouldn't recognize Him.)

Then **read** aloud John 1:14, 18. **Share: Jesus came to earth as a man so He could teach us about how much God loves us and wants us to have a relationship with Him.**

Close by having children thank God for sending Jesus at Christmas and for the promise of His return.

## WRAP-UP

Gather everyone in a circle and have family members take turns answering this question: **What's one thing you've learned about God today?**

Next, tell kids you've got a new "Life Slogan" you'd like to share with them.

**Life slogan: Today's Life Slogan is this: "Emmanuel, God is with us!"** Have family members repeat the slogan two or three times to help them learn it. Then encourage them to practice saying it during the week so they can talk about it at your next family night session.

**Close in Prayer:** Allow time for each family member to share prayer concerns and answers to prayer. Then close your time together with prayer for each concern. Thank God for listening to and caring about us.

Remember to record your prayer requests so you can refer to them in the future as you see God answering them.

## Additional Resources:

See page 86.

# How to Lead Your Child to Christ

## SOME THINGS TO CONSIDER AHEAD OF TIME:

1. Realize that God is more concerned about your child's eternal destiny and happiness than you are. "The Lord is not slow in keeping His promise. . . . He is patient with you, not wanting anyone to perish, but everyone to come to repentance" (2 Peter 3:9).

2. Pray specifically beforehand that God will give you insights and wisdom in dealing with each child on his or her maturity level.

3. Don't use terms like "take Jesus into your heart," "dying and going to hell," and "accepting Christ as your personal Savior." Children are either too literal ("How does Jesus breathe in my heart?") or the words are too clichéd and trite for their understanding.

4. Deal with each child alone, and don't be in a hurry. Make sure he or she understands. Discuss. Take your time.

## A FEW CAUTIONS:

1. When drawing children to Himself, Jesus said for others to "allow" them to come to Him (see Mark 10:14). Only with adults did He use the term "compel" (see Luke 14:23). Do not compel children.

2. Remember that unless the Holy Spirit is speaking to the child, there will be no genuine heart experience of regeneration. Parents, don't get caught up in the idea that Jesus will return the day before you were going to speak to your child about salvation and that it will be too late. Look at God's character— He *is* love! He is not dangling your child's soul over hell. Wait on God's timing.

    Pray with faith, believing. Be concerned, but don't push.

## THE PLAN:

1. **God loves you.** Recite John 3:16 with your child's name in place of "the world."

2. **Show the child his or her need of a Savior.**

   a. Deal with sin carefully. There is one thing that cannot enter heaven—sin.

   b. Be sure your child knows what sin is. Ask him to name some (things common to children—lying, sassing, disobeying, etc.). Sin is doing or thinking anything wrong according to God's Word. It is breaking God's Law.

   c. Ask the question "Have you sinned?" If the answer is no, do not continue. Urge him to come and talk to you again when he does feel that he has sinned. Dismiss him. You may want to have prayer first, however, thanking God "for this young child who is willing to do what is right." Make it easy for him to talk to you again, but do not continue. Do not say, "Oh, yes, you have too sinned!" and then name some. With children, wait for God's conviction.

   d. If the answer is yes, continue. He may even give a personal illustration of some sin he has done recently or one that has bothered him.

   e. Tell him what God says about sin: We've all sinned ("There is no one righteous, not even one," Rom. 3:10). And because of that sin, we can't get to God ("For the wages of sin is death . . . " Rom. 6:23). So He had to come to us (". . . but the gift of God is eternal life in Christ Jesus our Lord," Rom. 6:23).

   f. Relate God's gift of salvation to Christmas gifts—we don't earn them or pay for them; we just accept them and are thankful for them.

3. **Bring the child to a definite decision.**

   a. Christ must be received if salvation is to be possessed.

   b. Remember, do not force a decision.

   c. Ask the child to pray out loud in her own words. Give her some things she could say if she seems unsure. Now be prepared for a blessing! (It is best to avoid having the child repeat a memorized prayer after you. Let her think, and make it personal.)*

d. After salvation has occurred, pray for her out loud. This is a good way to pronounce a blessing on her.

4. **Lead your child into assurance.**

Show him that he will have to keep his relationship open with God through repentance and forgiveness (just like with his family or friends), but that God will always love him ("Never will I leave you; never will I forsake you," Heb. 13:5).

\* If you wish to guide your child through the prayer, here is some suggested language.

> *"Dear God, I know that I am a sinner [have child name specific sins he or she acknowledged earlier, such as lying, stealing, disobeying, etc.]. I know that Jesus died on the cross to pay for all my sins. I ask You to forgive me of my sins. I believe that Jesus died for me and rose from the dead, and I accept Him as my Savior. Thank You for loving me. In Jesus' name. Amen."*

# Cumulative Topical Index

| TOPIC | SCRIPTURE | WHAT YOU'LL NEED | WHERE TO FIND IT |
|---|---|---|---|
| The Acts of the Sinful Nature and the Fruit of the Spirit | Gal. 5:19-26 | 3x5 cards or paper, markers, and tape | IFN, p. 43 |
| Adding Value to Money through Saving Takes Time | Matt. 6:19-21 | Supplies for making cookies and a Bible | MMK, p. 89 |
| All Have Sinned | Rom. 3:23 | Raw eggs, bucket of water | BCB, p. 89 |
| All of Our Plans Should Match God's | Ps. 139:1-18 | Paper, pencils, markers, or crayons | MMK, p. 73 |
| Avoid Things That Keep Us from Growing | Eph. 4:14-15; Heb. 5:11-14 | Seeds, plants at various stages of growth or a garden or nursery to tour, Bible | CCQ, p. 77 |
| Bad Company Corrupts Good Character | 1 Cor. 15:33 | Small ball, string, slips of paper, pencil, yarn or masking tape, Bible | IFN, p. 103 |
| Be Thankful for Good Friends | | Bible, art supplies, markers | IFN, p. 98 |
| Being Content with What We Have | Phil. 4:11-13 | Bible | CCQ, p. 17 |
| Being Diligent Means Working Hard and Well | Gen. 39–41 | Bible, paper, a pencil and other supplies depending on jobs chosen | MMK, p. 64 |
| Being a Faithful Steward Means Managing God's Gifts Wisely | 1 Peter 4:10; Luke 19:12-26 | Graham crackers, peanut butter, thin stick pretzels, small marshmallows, and M & Ms® | MMK, p. 18 |
| Budgeting Means Making a Plan for Using Our Money | Jud. 6–7 | Table, large sheets or paper, and markers or crayons | MMK, p. 79 |
| Budgeting Means the Money Coming in Has to Equal the Money Going Out | Luke 14:28-35; Jud. 6–7 | Supply of beans, paper, pencil, and Bible | MMK, p. 80 |
| Change Helps Us Grow and Mature | Rom. 8:28-39 | Bible | WLS, p. 39 |

| TOPIC | SCRIPTURE | WHAT YOU'LL NEED | WHERE TO FIND IT |
|-------|-----------|------------------|------------------|
| Change Is Good | 1 Kings 17:8-16 | Jar or box for holding change, colored paper, tape, markers, Bible | MMK, p. 27 |
| Christ Is Who We Serve | Col. 3:23-24 | Paper, scissors, pens | IFN, p. 50 |
| Christians Should Be Joyful Each Day | James 3:22-23; Ps. 118:24 | Small plastic bottle, cork to fit bottle opening, water, vinegar, paper towel, Bible | CCQ, p. 67 |
| Commitment and Hard Work Are Needed to Finish Strong | Gen. 6:5-22 | Jigsaw puzzle, Bible | CCQ, p. 83 |
| The Consequence of Sin Is Death | Ps. 19:1-6 | Dominoes | BCB, p. 57 |
| Contentment Is the Secret to Happiness | Matt. 6:33 | Package of candies, a Bible | MMK, p. 51 |
| Creation | Gen. 1:1; Ps. 19:1-6; Rom. 1:20 | Nature book or video, Bible | IFN, p. 17 |
| David and Bathsheba | 2 Sam. 11:1–12:14 | Bible | BCB, p. 90 |
| Description of Heaven | Rev. 21:3-4, 10-27 | Bible, drawing supplies | BCB, p. 76 |
| Difficulty Can Help Us Grow | Jer. 32:17; Luke 18:27 | Bible, card game like Old Maid or Crazy Eights | CCQ, p. 33 |
| Discipline and Training Make Us Stronger | Prov. 4:23 | Narrow doorway, Bible | CCQ, p. 103 |
| Don't Be Yoked with Unbelievers | 2 Cor. 16:17–17:1 | Milk, food coloring | IFN, p. 105 |
| Don't Give Respect Based on Material Wealth | Eph. 6:1-8; 1 Peter 2:13-17; Ps. 119:17; James 2:1-2; 1 Tim. 4:12 | Large sheet of paper, tape, a pen, Bible | IFN, p. 64 |
| Easter Was God's Plan for Jesus | John 3:16; Rom. 3:23; 6:23 | Paper and pencils or pens, materials to make a large cross, and a Bible | HFN, p. 27 |
| Equality Does Not Mean Contentment | Matt. 20:1-16 | Money or candy bars, tape recorder or radio, Bible | WLS, p. 21 |
| Even if We're Not in the Majority, We May Be Right | 2 Tim. 3:12-17 | Piece of paper, pencil, water | CCQ, p. 95 |
| Every Day Is a Gift from God | Prov. 16:9 | Bible | CCQ, p. 69 |

AN INTRODUCTION TO FAMILY NIGHTS
= IFN

BASIC CHRISTIAN BELIEFS
= BCB

CHRISTIAN CHARACTER QUALITIES
= CCQ

WISDOM LIFE SKILLS
= WLS

MONEY MATTERS FOR KIDS
= MMK

HOLIDAYS
= HFN

AN
INTRODUCTION
TO FAMILY
NIGHTS
= IFN
· · · · · · · · · ·
BASIC
CHRISTIAN
BELIEFS
= BCB
· · · · · · · · · ·
CHRISTIAN
CHARACTER
QUALITIES
= CCQ
· · · · · · · · · ·
WISDOM LIFE
SKILLS
= WLS
· · · · · · · · · ·
MONEY
MATTERS FOR
KIDS
= MMK
· · · · · · · · · ·
HOLIDAYS
FAMILY NIGHT
= HFN

| TOPIC | SCRIPTURE | WHAT YOU'LL NEED | WHERE TO FIND IT |
|---|---|---|---|
| Evil Hearts Say Evil Words | Prov. 15:2-8; Luke 6:45; Eph. 4:29 | Bible, small mirror | IFN, p. 79 |
| The Fruit of the Spirit | Gal. 5:22-23; Luke 3:8; Acts 26:20 | Blindfold and Bible | BCB, p. 92 |
| God Allows Testing to Help Us Mature | James 1:2-4 | Bible | BCB, p. 44 |
| God Became a Man So We Could Understand His Love | John 14:9-10 | A pet of some kind, and a Bible | HFN, p. 85 |
| God Can Clean Our Guilty Consciences | 1 John 1:9 | Small dish of bleach, dark piece of material, Bible | WLS, p. 95 |
| God Can Do the Impossible | John 6:1-14 | Bible, sturdy plank (6 or more inches wide and 6 to 8 feet long), a brick or similar object, snack of fish and crackers | CCQ, p. 31 |
| God Can Guide Us Away from Satan's Traps | Ps. 119:9-11; Prov. 3:5-6 | Ten or more inexpensive mousetraps, pencil, blindfold, Bible | WLS, p. 72 |
| God Can Help Us Knock Sin Out of Our Lives | Ps. 32:1-5; 1 John 1:9 | Heavy drinking glass, pie tin, small slips of paper, pencils, large raw egg, cardboard tube from a roll of toilet paper, broom, masking tape, Bible | WLS, p. 53 |
| God Cares for Us Even in Hard Times | Job 1–2; 42 | Bible | WLS, p. 103 |
| God Chose to Make Dads (or Moms) as a Picture of Himself | Gen. 1:26-27 | Large sheets of paper, pencils, a bright light, a picture of your family, a Bible | HFN, p. 47 |
| God Created Us | Isa. 45:9, 64:8; Ps. 139:13 | Bible and video of potter with clay | BCB, p. 43 |
| God Doesn't Want Us to Worry | Matt. 6:25-34; Phil. 4:6-7; Ps. 55:22 | Bible, paper, pencils | CCQ, p. 39 |
| God Forgives Those Who Confess Their Sins | 1 John 1:9 | Sheets of paper, tape, Bible | BCB, p. 58 |
| God Gave Jesus a Message for Us | John 1:14,18; 8:19; 12:49-50 | Goldfish in water or bug in jar, water | BCB, p. 66 |
| God Gives and God Can Take Away | Luke 12:13-21 | Bible, timer with bell or buzzer, large bowl of small candies, smaller bowl for each child | CCQ, p. 15 |

| TOPIC | SCRIPTURE | WHAT YOU'LL NEED | WHERE TO FIND IT |
|---|---|---|---|
| God Is Holy | Ex. 3:1-6 | Masking tape, baby powder or corn starch, broom, Bible | IFN, p. 31 |
| God Is Invisible, Powerful, and Real | John 1:18, 4:24; Luke 24:36-39 | Balloons, balls, refrigerator magnets, Bible | IFN, p. 15 |
| God Knew His Plans for Us | Jer. 29:11 | Two puzzles and a Bible | BCB, p. 19 |
| God Knows All about Us | Ps. 139:2-4; Matt. 10:30 | 3x5 cards, a pen | BCB, p. 17 |
| God Knows Everything | Isa. 40:13-14; Eph. 4:1-6 | Bible | IFN, p. 15 |
| God Knows the Plan for Our Lives | Rom. 8:28 | Three different 25–50 piece jigsaw puzzles, Bible | WLS, p. 101 |
| God Looks beyond the Mask and into our Hearts | | Costumes | HFN, p. 65 |
| God Loves Us So Much, He Sent Jesus | John 3:16; Eph. 2:8-9 | I.O.U. for each family member | IFN, p. 34 |
| God Made Our Family Unique by Placing Each of Us in It | | Different color paint for each family member, toothpicks or paintbrushes to dip into paint, white paper, Bible | BCB, p. 110 |
| God Made Us | | Building blocks, such as Tinkertoys, Legos, or K'nex | HFN, p. 15 |
| God Made Us in His Image | Gen. 1:24-27 | Play dough or clay and Bible | BCB, p. 24 |
| God Never Changes | Ecc. 3:1-8; Heb. 13:8 | Paper, pencils, Bible | WLS, p. 37 |
| God Owns Everything; He Gives Us Things to Manage | | Large sheet of poster board or newsprint and colored markers | MMK, p. 17 |
| God Provides a Way Out of Temptation | 1 Cor. 10:12-13; James 1:13-14; 4:7; 1 John 2:15-17 | Bible | IFN, p. 88 |
| God Sees Who We Really Are—We Can Never Fool Him | 1 Sam. 16:7 | Construction paper, scissors, crayons or markers, a hat or bowl, and a Bible | HFN, p. 66 |
| God Teaches Us about Love through Others | 1 Cor. 13 | Colored paper, markers, crayons, scissors, tape or glue, and a Bible | HFN, p. 22 |
| God Wants Our Best Effort in All We Do | Col. 3:23-24 | Children's blocks or a large supply of cardboard boxes | MMK, p. 63 |

| TOPIC | SCRIPTURE | WHAT YOU'LL NEED | WHERE TO FIND IT |
|---|---|---|---|
| God Wants Us to Be Diligent in Our Work | Prov. 6:6-11; 1 Thes. 4:11-12 | Video about ants or picture books or encyclopedia, Bible | CCQ, p. 55 |
| God Wants Us to Get Closer to Him | James 4:8; 1 John 4:7-12 | Hidden Bibles, clues to find them | BCB, p. 33 |
| God Wants Us to Glorify Him | Ps. 24:1; Luke 12:13-21 | Paper, pencils, Bible | WLS, p. 47 |
| God Wants Us to Work and Be Helpful | 2 Thes. 3:6-15 | Several undone chores, Bible | CCQ, p. 53 |
| God Will Send the Holy Spirit | John 14:23-26; 1 Cor. 2:12 | Flashlights, small treats, Bible | IFN, p. 39 |
| God's Covenant with Noah | Gen. 8:13-21; 9:8-17 | Bible, paper, crayons or markers | BCB, p. 52 |
| Guarding the Gate to Our Minds | Prov. 4:13; 2 Cor. 11:3; Phil. 4:8 | Bible, poster board for each family member, old magazines, glue, scissors, markers | CCQ, p. 23 |
| The Holy Spirit Helps Us | Eph. 1:17; John 14:15-17; Acts 1:1-11; Eph. 3:16-17; Rom. 8:26-27; 1 Cor. 2:11-16 | Bible | BCB, p. 99 |
| Honesty Means Being Sure We Tell the Truth and Are Fair | Prov. 10:9; 11:3; 12:5; 14:2; 28:13 | A bunch of coins and a Bible | MMK, p. 58 |
| Honor the Holy Spirit, Don't Block Him | 1 John 4:4; 1 Cor. 6:19-20 | Bible, blow-dryer or vacuum cleaner with exit hose, a Ping-Pong ball | CCQ, p. 47 |
| Honor Your Parents | Ex. 20:12 | Paper, pencil, treats, umbrella, soft objects, masking tape, pen, Bible | IFN, p. 55 |
| If We Confess Our Sins, Jesus Will Forgive Us | Heb. 12:1; 1 John 1:9 | Magic slate, candies, paper, pencils, bathrobe ties or soft rope, items to weigh someone down, and a Bible | HFN, p. 28 |
| Investing and Saving Adds Value to Money | Prov. 21:20 | Two and a half dollars for each family member | MMK, p. 87 |
| It's Better to Follow the Truth | Rom. 1:25; Prov. 2:1-5 | Second set of clues, box of candy or treats, Bible | WLS, p. 86 |
| It's Better to Wait for Something Than to Borrow Money to Buy It | 2 Kings 4:1-7; Prov. 22:7 | Magazines, advertisements, paper, a pencil, Bible | MMK, p. 103 |

| TOPIC | SCRIPTURE | WHAT YOU'LL NEED | WHERE TO FIND IT |
| --- | --- | --- | --- |
| It's Difficult to Be a Giver When You're a Debtor | | Pennies or other coins | MMK, p. 105 |
| It's Easy to Follow a Lie, but It Leads to Disappointment | | Clues as described in lesson, empty box | WLS, p. 85 |
| The Importance of Your Name Being Written in the Book of Life | Rev. 20:11-15; 21:27 | Bible, phone book, access to other books with family name | BCB, p. 74 |
| It's Important to Listen to Jesus' Message | | Bible | BCB, p. 68 |
| Jesus Came to Die for Our Sins | Rom. 5:8 | A large piece of cardboard, markers, scissors, tape, and a Bible | HFN, p. 91 |
| Jesus Came to Give Us Eternal Life | Mark 16:12-14 | A calculator, a calendar, a sheet of paper, and a pencil | HFN, p. 91 |
| Jesus Came to Teach Us about God | John 1:14, 18 | Winter clothing, bread crumbs, a Bible | HFN, p. 92 |
| Jesus Came to Show Us How Much God Loves Us | John 3:16 | Supplies to make an Advent wreath, and a Bible | HFN, p. 89 |
| Jesus Died for Our Sins | Luke 22:1-6; Mark 14:12-26; Luke 22:47-54; Luke 22:55-62; Matt. 27:1-10; Matt. 27:11-31; Luke 23:26-34 | Seven plastic eggs, slips of paper with Scripture verses, and a Bible | HFN, p. 33 |
| Jesus Dies on the Cross | John 14:6 | 6-foot 2x4, 3-foot 2x4, hammers, nails, Bible | IFN, p. 33 |
| Jesus Promises Us New Bodies and a New Home in Heaven | Phil. 3:20-21; Luke 24:36-43; Rev. 21:1-4 | Ingredients for making pumpkin pie, and a Bible | HFN, p. 61 |
| Jesus Took Our Sins to the Cross and Freed Us from Being Bound Up in Sin | Rom. 6:23, 5:8; 6:18 | Soft rope or heavy yarn, a watch with a second hand, thread, and a Bible | HFN, p. 53 |
| Jesus Took the Punishment We Deserve | Rom. 6:23; John 3:16; Rom. 5:8-9 | Bathrobe, list of bad deeds | IFN, p. 26 |
| Jesus Was Victorious Over Death and Sin | Luke 23:35-43; Luke 23:44-53; Matt. 27:59-61; Luke 23:54–24:12 | Five plastic eggs— four with Scripture verses, and a Bible | HFN, p. 36 |

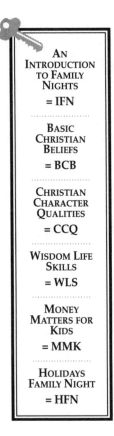

An
Introduction
to Family
Nights
= IFN

Basic
Christian
Beliefs
= BCB

Christian
Character
Qualities
= CCQ

Wisdom Life
Skills
= WLS

Money
Matters for
Kids
= MMK

Holidays
Family Night
= HFN

Heritage
BUILDERS

| TOPIC | SCRIPTURE | WHAT YOU'LL NEED | WHERE TO FIND IT |
|---|---|---|---|
| Jesus Washes His Followers' Feet | John 13:1-17 | Bucket of warm soapy water, towels, Bible | IFN, p. 63 |
| Joshua and the Battle of Jericho | Josh. 1:16-18; 6:1-21 | Paper, pencil, dots on paper that, when connected, form a star | IFN, p. 57 |
| Knowing God's Word Helps Us Know What Stand to Take | 2 Tim. 3:1-5 | Current newspaper, Bible | CCQ, p. 93 |
| Look to God, Not Others | Phil. 4:11-13 | Magazines or newspapers, a chair, several pads of small yellow stickies, Bible | WLS, p. 24 |
| Love Is Unselfish | 1 Cor. 13 | A snack and a Bible | HFN, p. 21 |
| Loving Money Is Wrong | 1 Tim. 6:6-10 | Several rolls of coins, masking tape, Bible | WLS, p. 45 |
| Lying Can Hurt People | Acts 5:1-11 | Two pizza boxes—one empty and one with a fresh pizza—and a Bible | MMK, p. 57 |
| Meeting Goals Requires Planning | Prov. 3:5-6 | Paper, scissors, pencils, a treat, a Bible | MMK, p. 71 |
| Moms Are Special and Important to Us and to God | Prov. 24:3-4 | Confetti, streamers, a comfortable chair, a wash basin with warm water, two cloths, and a Bible | HFN, p. 41 |
| Moms Model Jesus' Love When They Serve Gladly | 2 Tim. 1:4-7 | Various objects depending on chosen activity and a Bible | HFN, p. 42 |
| The More We Know God, the More We Know His Voice | John 10:1-6 | Bible | BCB, p. 35 |
| Nicodemus Asks Jesus about Being Born Again | John 3:7, 50-51; 19:39-40 | Bible, paper, pencil, costume | BCB, p. 81 |
| Obedience Has Good Rewards | | Planned outing everyone will enjoy, directions on 3x5 cards, number cards | IFN, p. 59 |
| Only a Relationship with God Can Fill Our Need | Isa. 55:1-2 | Doll that requires batteries, batteries for the doll, dollar bill, pictures of a house, an expensive car, and a pretty woman or handsome man, Bible | WLS, p. 62 |

| TOPIC | SCRIPTURE | WHAT YOU'LL NEED | WHERE TO FIND IT |
|---|---|---|---|
| Our Conscience Helps Us Know Right from Wrong | Rom. 2:14-15 | Foods with a strong smell, blindfold, Bible | WLS, p. 93 |
| Our Minds Should Be Filled with Good, Not Evil | Phil 4:8; Ps. 119:9, 11 | Bible, bucket of water, several large rocks | CCQ, p. 26 |
| Parable of the Talents | Matt. 25:14-30 | Bible | IFN, p. 73 |
| Parable of the Vine and Branches | John 15:1-8 | Tree branch, paper, pencils, Bible | IFN, p. 95 |
| Persecution Brings a Reward | | Bucket, bag of ice, marker, one-dollar bill | WLS, p. 32 |
| Planning Helps Us Finish Strong | Phil. 3:10-14 | Flight map on p. 86, paper, pencils, Bible | CCQ, p. 85 |
| Pray, Endure, and Be Glad When We're Persecuted | Matt. 5:11-12, 44; Rom. 12:14; 1 Cor. 4:12 | Notes, Bible, candle or flashlight, dark small space | WLS, p. 29 |
| The Responsibilities of Families | Eph. 5:22-33; 6:1-4 | Photo albums, Bible | BCB, p. 101 |
| Satan Looks for Ways to Trap Us | Luke 4:1-13 | Cardboard box, string, stick, small ball, Bible | WLS, p. 69 |
| Self-control Helps Us Resist the Enemy | 1 Peter 5:8-9; 1 Peter 2:11-12 | Blindfold, watch or timer, feather or other "tickly" item, Bible | CCQ, p. 101 |
| Serve One Another in Love | Gal. 5:13 | Bag of small candies, at least three per child | IFN, p. 47 |
| Sin and Busyness Interfere with Our Prayers | Luke 10:38-42; Ps. 46:10; Matt. 5:23-24; 1 Peter 3:7 | Bible, two paper cups, two paper clips, long length of fishing line | CCQ, p. 61 |
| Sin Separates Humanity | Gen. 3:1-24 | Bible, clay creations, piece of hardened clay or play dough | BCB, p. 25 |
| Some Places Aren't Open to Everyone | | Book or magazine with "knock-knock" jokes | BCB, p. 73 |
| Some Things in Life Are Out of Our Control | | Blindfolds | BCB, p. 41 |
| Temptation Takes Our Eyes Off God | | Fishing pole, items to catch, timer, Bible | IFN, p. 85 |
| There Is a Difference Between Needs and Wants | Prov. 31:16; Matt. 6:21 | Paper, pencils, glasses of drinking water, a soft drink | MMK, p. 95 |
| Those Who Don't Believe Are Foolish | Ps. 44:1 | Ten small pieces of paper, pencil, Bible | IFN, p. 19 |

AN INTRODUCTION TO FAMILY NIGHTS
= IFN

BASIC CHRISTIAN BELIEFS
= BCB

CHRISTIAN CHARACTER QUALITIES
= CCQ

WISDOM LIFE SKILLS
= WLS

MONEY MATTERS FOR KIDS
= MMK

HOLIDAYS
= HFN

AN
INTRODUCTION
TO FAMILY
NIGHTS
= IFN

BASIC
CHRISTIAN
BELIEFS
= BCB

CHRISTIAN
CHARACTER
QUALITIES
= CCQ

WISDOM LIFE
SKILLS
= WLS

MONEY
MATTERS FOR
KIDS
= MMK

HOLIDAYS
FAMILY NIGHT
= HFN

| TOPIC | SCRIPTURE | WHAT YOU'LL NEED | WHERE TO FIND IT |
|---|---|---|---|
| Tithing Means Giving One-Tenth Back to God | Gen. 28:10-22; Ps. 3:9-10 | All family members need ten similar items each, a Bible | MMK, p. 33 |
| The Tongue Is Small but Powerful | James 3:3-12 | Video, news magazine or picture book showing devastation of fire, match, candle, Bible | IFN, p. 77 |
| The Treasure of a Thankful Heart Is Contentment | Eph. 5:20 | 3x5 cards, pencils, fun prizes, and a Bible | HFN, p. 72 |
| Trials Help Us Grow | James 1:2-4 | Sugar cookie dough, cookie cutters, baking sheets, miscellaneous baking supplies, Bible | WLS, p. 15 |
| Trials Test How We've Grown | James 1:12 | Bible | WLS, p. 17 |
| Trust Is Important | Matt. 6:25-34 | Each person needs an item he or she greatly values | MMK, p. 25 |
| We All Sin | Rom. 3:23 | Target and items to throw | IFN, p. 23 |
| We Are Made in God's Image | Gen. 2:7; Ps. 139:13-16 | Paper bags, candies, a Bible, supplies for making gingerbread cookies | HFN, p. 17 |
| We Become a New Creation When Jesus Comes into Our Hearts | Matt. 23:25-28; Rev. 3:20; 2 Cor. 5:17; Eph. 2:10; 2 Cor. 4:7-10; Matt. 5:14-16; 2 Cor. 4:6 | Pumpkin, newspaper, sharp knife, a spoon, a candle, matches, and a Bible | HFN, p. 59 |
| We Can Communicate with Each Other | | | BCB, p. 65 |
| We Can Fight the Temptation to Want More Stuff | Matt. 4:1-11; Heb. 13:5 | Television, paper, a pencil, Bible | MMK, p. 49 |
| We Can Give Joyfully to Others | Luke 10:25-37 | Bible, soft yarn | MMK, p. 41 |
| We Can Help Each Other | Prov. 27:17 | Masking tape, bowl of unwrapped candies, rulers, yardsticks, or dowel rods | BCB, p. 110 |
| We Can Help People When We Give Generously | 2 Cor. 6–7 | Variety of supplies, depending on chosen activity | MMK, p. 43 |
| We Can Learn about God from Mom (or Dad) | | Supplies to make a collage (magazines, paper, tape or glue, scissors) | HFN, p. 49 |

| TOPIC | SCRIPTURE | WHAT YOU'LL NEED | WHERE TO FIND IT |
|---|---|---|---|
| We Can Love by Helping Those in Need | Heb. 13:1-3 | | IFN, p. 48 |
| We Can Show Love through Respecting Family Members | | Paper and pen | IFN, p. 66 |
| We Can't Take Back the Damage of Our Words | | Tube of toothpaste for each child, $10 bill | IFN, p. 78 |
| We Deserve Punishment for Our Sins | Rom. 6:23 | Dessert, other materials as decided | IFN, p. 24 |
| We Give to God because We're Thankful | | Supplies for a celebration dinner, also money for each family member | MMK, p. 36 |
| We Have All We Need in Our Lives | Ecc. 3:11 | Paper, pencils, Bible | WLS, p. 61 |
| We Have a New Life in Christ | John 3:3; 2 Cor. 5:17 | Video or picture book of caterpillar forming a cocoon then a butterfly, or a tadpole becoming a frog, or a seed becoming a plant | BCB, p. 93 |
| We Have Much to Be Thankful For | 1 Chron. 16:4-36 | Unpopped popcorn, a bowl, supplies for popping popcorn, and a Bible | HFN, p. 79 |
| We Know Others by Our Relationships with Them | | Copies of question-naire, pencils, Bible | BCB, p. 31 |
| We Must Be in Constant Contact with God | | Blindfold | CCQ, p. 63 |
| We Must Choose to Obey | | 3x5 cards or slips of paper, markers, and tape | IFN, p. 43 |
| We Must Either Choose Christ or Reject Christ | Matt. 12:30 | Clear glass jar, cooking oil, water, spoon, Bible | CCQ, p. 96 |
| We Must Give Thanks in All Circumstances | 1 Thes. 5:18 | A typical family meal, cloth strips, and a Bible | HFN, p. 77 |
| We Must Learn How Much Responsibility We Can Handle | | Building blocks, watch with second hand, paper, pencil | IFN, p. 71 |
| We Must Listen | Prov. 1:5, 8-9; 4:1 | Bible, other supplies for the task you choose | WLS, p. 77 |

Family Night
TOOL CHEST

AN INTRODUCTION TO FAMILY NIGHTS
= IFN

BASIC CHRISTIAN BELIEFS
= BCB

CHRISTIAN CHARACTER QUALITIES
= CCQ

WISDOM LIFE SKILLS
= WLS

MONEY MATTERS FOR KIDS
= MMK

HOLIDAYS
= HFN

| TOPIC | SCRIPTURE | WHAT YOU'LL NEED | WHERE TO FIND IT |
|---|---|---|---|
| We Must Think Before We Speak | James 1:19 | Bible | WLS, p. 79 |
| We Need to Grow Physically, Emotionally, and Spiritually | 1 Peter 2:2 | Photograph albums or videos of your children at different ages, tape measure, bathroom scale, Bible | CCQ, p. 75 |
| We Prove Who We Are When What We Do Reflects What We Say | James 1:22; 2:14-27 | A bag of candy, a rope, and a Bible | HFN, p. 67 |
| We Reap What We Sow | Gal. 6:7 | Candy bar, Bible | IFN, p. 55 |
| We Shouldn't Value Possessions Over Everything Else | 1 Tim. 6:7-8 | Box is optional | CCQ, p. 18 |
| When God Sent Jesus to Earth, God Chose Me | Luke 1:26-38; John 3:16; Matt. 14:23 | Going to choose a Christmas tree or other special decoration, a Bible, and hot chocolate | HFN, p. 83 |
| When We Focus on What We Don't Have, We Get Unhappy | 1 Tim. 6:9-10; 1 Thes. 5:18; Phil. 4:11-13 | A glass, water, paper, crayons, and a Bible | HFN, p. 71 |
| When We're Set Free from Sin, We Have the Freedom to Choose, and the Responsibility to Serve | Gal. 5:13-15 | Candies, soft rope, and a Bible | HFN, p. 55 |
| Wise Spending Means Getting Good Value for What We Buy | Luke 15:11-32 | Money and a Bible | MMK, p. 97 |
| With Help, Life Is a Lot Easier | | Supplies to do the chore you choose | BCB, p. 101 |
| Wolves in Sheeps' Clothing | Matt. 7:15-20 | Ten paper sacks, a marker, ten small items, Bible | IFN, p. 97 |
| Worrying Doesn't Change Anything | | Board, inexpensive doorbell buzzer, a 9-volt battery, extra length of electrical wire, a large belt, assorted tools | CCQ, p. 37 |
| You Look Like the Person in Whose Image You Are Created | | Paper roll, crayons, markers, pictures of your kids and of yourself as a child | BCB, p. 23 |

# Welcome to the Family!

## Heritage Builders

*Helping You Build a Family of Faith*

We hope you've enjoyed this book. Heritage Builders was founded in 1995 by three fathers with a passion for the next generation. As a new ministry of Focus on the Family, Heritage Builders strives to equip, train and motivate parents to become intentional about building a strong spiritual heritage.

It's quite a challenge for busy parents to find ways to build a spiritual foundation for their families—especially in a way they enjoy and understand. Through activities and participation, children can learn biblical truth in a way they can understand, enjoy—and *remember.*

Passing along a heritage of Christian faith to your family is a parent's highest calling. Heritage Builders' goal is to encourage and empower you in this great mission with practical resources and inspiring ideas that really work—and help your children develop a lasting love for God.

\*\*\*

## How To Reach Us

For more information, visit our Heritage Builders Web site! Log on to **www.heritagebuilders.com** to discover new resources, sample activities, and ideas to help you pass on a spiritual heritage. To request any of these resources, simply call Focus on the Family at 1-800-A-FAMILY (1-800-232-6459) or in Canada, call 1-800-661-9800. Or send your request to Focus on the Family, Colorado Springs, CO 80995. In Canada, write Focus on the Family, P.O. Box 9800, Stn. Terminal, Vancouver, B.C. V6B 4G3

To learn more about Focus on the Family or to find out if there is an associate office in your country, please visit www. family.org

We'd love to hear from you!

# Try These Heritage Builders Resources!

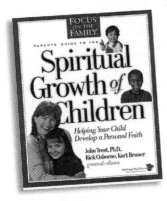

## Parents' Guide to the Spiritual Growth of Children

Building a foundation of faith in your children can be easy–and fun!–with help from the *Parents' Guide to the Spiritual Growth of Children*. Through simple and practical advice, this comprehensive guide shows you how to build a spiritual training plan for your family and it explains what to teach your children at different ages.

## Bedtime Blessings

Strengthen the precious bond between you, your child and God by making *Bedtime Blessings* a special part of your evenings together. From best-selling author John Trent, Ph.D., and Heritage Builders, this book is filled with stories, activities and blessing prayers to help you practice the biblical model of "blessing."

## My Time With God

Send your child on an amazing adventure—a self-guided tour through God's Word! *My Time With God* shows your 8- to 12-year-old how to get to know God regularly in exciting ways. Through 150 days' worth of fun facts and mind-boggling trivia, prayer starters, and interesting questions, your child will discover how awesome God really is!

## The Singing Bible

Children ages 2 to 7 will love *The Singing Bible,* which sets the Bible to music with over 50 fun, sing-along songs! Lead your child through Scripture by using *The Singing Bible* to introduce the story of Jonah, the Ten Commandments and more. This is a fun, fast-paced journey kids will remember!

• • •

Visit our Heritage Builders Web site! Log on to **www.heritagebuilders.com** to discover new resources, sample activities, and ideas to help you pass on a spiritual heritage. To request any of these resources, simply call Focus on the Family at 1-800-A-FAMILY (1-800-232-6459) or in Canada, call 1-800-661-9800. Or send your request to Focus on the Family, Colorado Springs, CO 80995. In Canada, write Focus on the Family, P.O. Box 9800, Stn. Terminal, Vancouver, B.C. V6B 4G3.

Heritage Builders™

*Helping You Build a Family of Faith*

Every family has a heritage—a spiritual, emotional, and social legacy passed from one generation to the next. There are four main areas we at Heritage Builders recommend parents consider as they plan to pass their faith to their children:

### Family Fragrance

Every family's home has a fragrance. Heritage Builders encourages parents to create a home environment that fosters a sweet, Christ-centered AROMA of love through Affection, Respect, Order, Merriment, and Affirmation.

### Family Traditions

Whether you pass down stories, beliefs and/or customs, traditions can help you establish a special identity for your family. Heritage Builders encourages parents to set special "milestones" for their children to help guide them and move them through their spiritual development.

### Family Compass

Parents have the unique task of setting standards for normal, healthy living through their attitudes, actions and beliefs. Heritage Builders encourages parents to give their children the moral navigation tools they need to succeed on the roads of life.

### Family Moments

Creating special, teachable moments with their children is one of a parent's most precious and sometimes, most difficult responsibilities. Heritage Builders encourages parents to capture little moments throughout the day to teach and impress values, beliefs, and biblical principles onto their children.

We look forward to standing alongside you as you seek to impart the Lord's care and wisdom onto the next generation—onto your children.

Heritage
Builders
*Helping You Build a Family of Faith*